I've Got a Domain Name—Now What???

A Practical Guide to Building a Website and Your Web Presence

By
Jean Bedord

20660 Stevens Creek Blvd., Suite 210
Cupertino, CA 95014

First Printing: November 2008
Second Printing: August 2010
Paperback ISBN: 1-60005-109-X (978-1-60005-109-8)
Place of Publication: Silicon Valley, California, USA
Paperback Library of Congress Number: 2008941051
eBook ISBN: 1-60005-110-3 (978-1-60005-110-4)

Trademarks

Warning and Disclaimer

Praise for this Book

"A great primer for any person putting up their first web presence or getting familiar with the terminology to make intelligent decisions when working with web design professionals."
Vitaly M. Golomb, CEO, Sputnik Ecommerce

"'I've got a Domain Name—Now What???' helps readers understand why it is important to have a domain for professional and personal pursuits and how to manage the development phase of the process without feeling overwhelmed. Throughout each chapter, Jean breaks the web development tasks into easy to understand steps with realistic time frames for completion. Whether you are considering purchasing a domain name to manage your career, launch a business, or build a specialized community, this book is a 'must read'."
Barbara Safani, CEO, Career Solvers and Author of 'Happy About My Resume'

"This is a great book for anyone who is ready to jump into the online world the right way but doesn't know what they need. Getting free hosting doesn't cut it, and Jean shares with you step-by-step tactics to get your business up and running on the web."
Jason Alba, CEO of JibberJobber.com

"In less than 100 pages author Jean Bedord demystifies website development. The step-by-step action plan outlined in the final chapter alone makes this a 'must have' for getting up and running on the Web."
Cindy Shamel, Shamel Information Services,
http://shamelinfo.com

"An invaluable resource to getting your website up the right way the first time."
Kristy Rogers, eWomenNetwork, San Jose
http://ewomennetwork.com/chapter/sanjose

"Step by step, Jean Bedord will lead you through what you have to do to create and build up your web presence. Jean is a practical and hands-on professional and she knows how to present material in a way that is easy to understand. For the beginner do-it-yourselfer, as well as for someone who wants to know how to talk to outside website developers, Jean has the answers."
Patricia Joseph, CEO, Prospex Information

Author

- Jean Bedord
  http://econtentstrategies.com

Publisher

- Mitchell Levy
  http://happyabout.com

Edit and Content Layout

- Teclarity
  http://teclarity.com

Cover Design

- Cate Calson
  http://calsongraphics.com

Dedication

To my husband, son and extended family and their tolerance of the hours I spend on the computer.

Acknowledgments

This book is the result of many, many conversations and emails with my friends and colleagues who are business savvy and familiar with technology in their day-to-day work. Yet they struggle to put the pieces together to make web technology work for their lives outside the technical structure provided by their organizations. Many have figured out how to register a domain name, and set up email, but not how to send email with their own domain name. They agonize for months, even years, over setting up a website, not realizing they can use simple "starter" approaches.

It was their questions that led me to this guide, so others don't have to go through the same learning curve I had to master. My thanks to the many techies who tolerated my questions on how these web technologies really work together.

And special thanks to Pat Wiklund who helped me develop the voice to translate these technologies into everyday English.

A Message from Happy About®

Thank you for your purchase of this Happy About book. It is available online at http://happyabout.com/ivegotadomainname.php or at other online and physical bookstores.

- Please contact us for quantity discounts at sales@happyabout.info
- If you want to be informed by email of upcoming Happy About® books, please email bookupdate@happyabout.info

Happy About is interested in you if you are an author who would like to submit a non-fiction book proposal or a corporation that would like to have a book written for you. Please contact us by email at editorial@happyabout.info or phone 408-257-3000.

Other Happy About books available include:

- 42 Rules™ of Marketing:
  http://happyabout.com/42rules/marketing.php
- 42 Rules™ of Social Media for Business:
  http://happyabout.com/42rules/social-media-business.php
- 42 Rules™ for 24-Hour Success on LinkedIn:
  http://happyabout.com/42rules/24hr-success-linkedin.php
- I'm On LinkedIn—Now What???:
  http://happyabout.com/linkedinhelp.php
- I'm on Facebook—Now What???:
  http://happyabout.com/facebook.php
- Twitter Means Business:
  http://happyabout.com/twitter/tweet2success.php
- Collaboration 2.0:
  http://happyabout.com/collaboration2.0.php
- The Emergence of The Relationship Economy:
  http://happyabout.com/RelationshipEconomy.php
- The Successful Introvert:
  http://happyabout.com/thesuccessfulintrovert.php
- Happy About Customer Service:
  http://happyabout.com/customerservice.php
- Care: You Have the Power!:
  http://happyabout.com/care.php
- Confessions of a Resilient Entrepreneur:
  http://happyabout.com/confessions-entrepreneur.php
- DNA of the Young Entrepreneur:
  http://happyabout.com/dna.php

Contents

1 Understanding the Domain Name System

Why are Domain Names Needed?

The world wide web has changed our lives in many ways. Searching the web and sending email are now part of our day-to-day lives. Organizations are expected to have websites. Professionals put their portfolios out on the web to attract new clients. Businesses use web technologies to sell products and provide customer service. Students learn to build websites in school.

Building and having a web presence is now part of everyday conversation. We used to ask for phone number and address—now we ask for email and website. Our children assume all information is on the web, and is immediately available. They don't look up information in the white pages or yellow pages or other traditional sources; instead they go to known sites or use search engines.

The Domain Name System (DNS) provides the architecture that allows computers to communicate with each other, and is the very foundation of the web. The concept is straightforward. Interconnected computers have numeric IP (Internet Protocol) addresses, but these are not easy for people to remember. DNS solves this problem.

Established in the 1980s, DNS is essentially a master registry of human-readable addresses assigned to the numeric IP codes that computers understand. DNS is like a phone book. Your listing in the phone book displays your name and your telephone number. People look you up by name to find your telephone number. Just as your name in the phone book is matched with a number, your phone number, similarly the domain name (sometimes simply called domain) is matched with the numeric IP address of an associated computer.

Every time you type in a web address or send an email, you are using domains controlled by some person or organization. Domains are deceptively simple. You recognize them as the characters that follow the @ in an email address. The structure is more complex than appears on the surface, and is used in different ways:

- Registered domain with a registrar*: example.com

- Email: yourname@example.com

- Domain name for a website: www.example.com

- URL (Uniform Resource Locator)
  http://www.example.com/index.html

The domain you use is your address on the web. It functions in ways similar to snail mail delivered to a mailbox at your physical address. You have multiple lives, so you can have multiple addresses:

- A work address which depends on your staying employed with that organization

- A home address which changes when you move to another residence

---

* A registrar, in this case, is a company that is authorized to register internet domain names.

- An virtual office service in a desirable location for your at-home business

- A post office box since you live in an apartment complex

- An address with a non-profit organization to which you belong

The physical location carries an implicit message. Notice how you react differently to these addresses:

- 1234 Park Avenue, New York, New York

- Rural Route 1, Boulder, Colorado

- Number 65, Chawan Road, Chengdu, Sichuan, Peoples' Republic of China

Likewise, a P.O. box address is sufficient for an independent writer, but doesn't convey substance for a business.

The same principles apply to the web world. The domain you use in the digital world carries a message like a street address in the physical world. Let's look at some common domain addresses and the implicit message:

- yourname@comcast.net is the equivalent of renting a P.O. box. This domain name says you have broadband access. This address, however, goes away with no automatic forwarding when you change your internet service provider, or ISP.

- yourname@aol.com is another common address. This was the format of my first email address. It worked for my family, since we could have up to six different email addresses, while paying for only one dial-up account. Now that AOL mail is free and I use a broadband service provider, I continue to keep those email addresses for my family and for testing purposes. There is also the "keeping in touch" factor—some of my former colleagues and relatives have never switched to my newer email accounts. Sometimes an AOL email can carry a mixed message depending on the context. For example, AOL email may indicate a senior executive with longevity in the online world, who prefers to maintain a personal account separate from her business account.

- Your.Name@youremployer.com is the format of your current business address. All business conveyed on behalf of your employer goes to this address. Personal mail sent to your business address is risky. Employers can choose to block incoming email from certain domains. Liability issues for employers are now a concern, since all email is archived, and may be subjected to legal e-discovery. Using a company email carries an additional down-side—it goes away if you are no longer working for that employer. And employers don't forward email to their ex-employees. Unexpectedly losing your job can mean losing contact with references and colleagues, and having to recreate those email contacts.

- Your.Name@university.edu is typical for college students and faculty. As a part-time faculty member in a distance education program, I use the university domain name to send email to my students, rather than using my other identities, so students will recognize the communication. Students usually lose this email address after leaving school, though sometimes alumni are encouraged to keep their university related email addresses. Stanford University continues its relationship and brand with alumni by providing emails of the form yourname@stanfordalumni.edu, which carries more cachet than other email domains.

- Your.ID@hotmail.com is an email account with Hotmail, a popular web mail service. Hotmail was the one of the earliest free email services and includes advertising. It screams "free," is often used for questionable activities, and not a legitimate business address. Deliverability can be an issue since some domains automatically screen out all Hotmail users.

Notice that all of these domains belong to someone else. They control the address where you receive your virtual mail. The corresponding website carries *their* brand identity, not yours.

The alternative is to own your own domain. Technically, this means you purchase the right to use a particular domain name for an annual fee. Owning a domain name now runs around $10 a year for basic registration, down from the initial $35+ annual fees. So the cost of building your own web presence is minimal.

What are the Advantages of Your Own Domain?

Owning your domain name gives you control of your email and your presence on the web. A domain provides a permanent address that is easy to remember and doesn't change with physical relocations and job changes. You can then use this address to develop your website property. Your electronic mail is delivered to the mailbox set up for that (virtual) location.

Let's examine how this works. You get a domain name from a domain name registrar who manages the domain for you in the master registry (similar to your phone listing in the white pages of the phone book) and handles the billing. I purchased the domain name "econtentstrategies.com" for my consulting business.

The first step in establishing my web presence was setting up emails to use my domain name. I created several emails, each for different purposes:

- JB@econtentstrategies.com for my business cards

- Pat@econtentstrategies.com for an advisor

- info@econtentstrategies.com to use for information queries

- whitepaper@econtentestrategies.com for a special offer

- accounting@econtentstrategies.com for a more professional image in sending and receiving invoices

Each of these email addresses that I created was an alias, or virtual address. This means that, behind the scenes, I control the forwarding of these addresses to other physical addresses which can be jbedord@aol.com or myaccount@comcast.net or myname@yahoo.com or any other physical email address. This worked well for me in the dotcom era when my ISP, @home.com, went out of business. The replacement was myname@attbi.com but this email didn't work smoothly the first week. Even worse, emails sent to myname@home.com did not get forwarded to myname@attbi.com—they bounced back to the sender as a bad email address. (Fortunately, when @attbi.com became @comcast.net, email addresses were migrated to the new domain.)

By using my domain, I was able to redirect all the incoming email to my AOL account until the email services stabilized. No lost communication with colleagues and clients. No new business cards. No need to notify everyone about a change of address.

They continued to see JB@econtentstrategies.com, not the invisible ISP redirects behind the scenes.

My second step in establishing a web presence was to use URL forwarding to a starter web page that could be used while I developed a more extensive website. Social media profiles didn't exist ten years ago, so I used AOL Hometown, available to me as a paying AOL subscriber. I could have used geocities.com or one of several other one-page services.

Then I printed up business cards with my email and website, and start marketing my services. My cost was only the registration fee, about $20 at that point. Low cost yet high value, the business logic of having your own domain is indisputable.

Choosing a Domain Name

Start by registering a personal domain that you can live with indefinitely, regardless of relocations and job changes. Variations of names work well, since this means aunts, uncles and cousins as well as friends and colleagues are likely to remember how to spell it. I registered jeanbedord.com, and since my name is commonly misspelled, also registered jeanbedford.com. So I have three domain registrations, which can forward mail to a single email inbox:

- Jean@Bedord.com as my family surname

- Jean@jeanbedord.com for my professional portfolio

- Jean@jeanbedford.com the misspelling to be redirected to my correct name

Registering a general family domain allows everyone in the family to have their own email address with the same domain. You can choose a domain like SmithEnterprises.com or SmithFamily.com. You can use this domain name for business cards for personal use, e.g. social gatherings and fishbowls for restaurant drawings.

My family uses bedord.com to stay in touch. I use econtentstrategies.com strictly for business, but also developed a website at www.JustAskJean.com for recommendations.

Branding is the major issue for choosing a domain name for a business, since it is used for both the website and email. Typically, it is the business name or its variation.

On the web, a one-person business can look as professional as a large company. The domain name is part of the URL (Uniform Resource Locator) used by search engines, so your business website can be found in a web search. The domain name gets incorporated into offline and online marketing, as well as day-to-day email communication. Therefore, your choice of domain name requires the same careful consideration as any other business decision.

Professionals and businesses carefully consider their street addresses, and the same principle applies to selecting domain names. A dentist can use something like smithdentistry.com, which can appear in print as SmithDentistry.com. A real estate agent could choose jonesrealestate.com which can become JonesRealEstate.com on a business card. (Search engines and web browsers ignore capitalization.) You need to look at the representation with and without capitals. It's hard for me to see the "v" in "mindyvhillman.com." Abbreviations can be problematic—"corp" or "corporation" or "Inc." are irrelevant to your brand, so I can't remember them as part of a domain name. Look carefully to see if a different capitalization changes the meaning, for example, the deceptively innocuous PenIsland.com.

You also need a domain name that's easy to say to another person without spelling it out. I had originally registered several "wrangler" domain names, but realized the spelling was not intuitively obvious outside the western U.S. Same problem with "cache" which is easily confused with "cash." This becomes particularly important for radio and television interviews and marketing.

Multiple Domain Scenarios

Chances are you will register more than one domain. I registered four when I first started; one for my business and three that were variations of my name. This happens all the time. If you had more than one property or more than one business, these would have different addresses. Some domains will be used for primary websites, but others are used for special purposes. So you, too, will probably need multiple domains. Let's look at some common scenarios for registering multiple domains:

- A bride and groom planning a wedding in San Francisco want to share their plans with family and friends, by creating a website with links to their gift registry, Flickr pictures, lodging information and local activities for those flying into the Bay Area.

- A weekend entrepreneur wants to test new business names by buying Pay Per Click (PPC) advertising on Google and measuring click-through rates.

- A mom has an interest in yoga and gardening. She develops two different part-time businesses, each with their own domain names.

- A volunteer for a youth soccer team gets a domain name for the league to send email to the players and their parents, and to develop an informational website.

- A school obtains a domain name to put up a website tracking progress on its annual fund-raising efforts.

- A real estate management company has several properties. Each property has its own website with location, pictures and tenant application procedures.

- An internet marketer is promoting a product and purchases a value-based domain name to use in advertising.

- A publisher has several publications, so each publication has its own domain name and mini-website, in addition to the main domain name for the company itself.

- An annual conference frequently has its own website with the name of the conference, which is then linked to the organizing company.

- A marketing department is offering a free report. Postcards will be mailed out with a report specific landing page with an easy-to-read domain name, not the company domain name.

Domains, as you see, can be useful for a number of purposes, and they can easily proliferate, much like the number of computers in our lives. There are the all-purpose computers and the *oh-so-specialized* versions to control our houses and vehicles. Now let's get started on staking out new properties....

MAIN DNS

bhhEnterprises
bhh Works

SUB DNS

bhh Photography Works
bhh Carpentry Works

TLD
(TOP LEVEL DOMAIN)

. com
. net
- org

Chapter 1: Understanding the Domain Name System

2 Registering a Domain

Where Do I Obtain a Domain?

Domain registrations are obtained from domain name registrars, who provide other services in addition to registry services. Registering a domain name entitles you to the right to use that domain for a period of time. The minimum is one year, and can be up to ten years. Let's look at how the domain name service works.

Information on the web resides on millions of computers scattered around the world. These computers are identified by IP (Internet Protocol) addresses that have a hard-to-remember numeric structure like 216.115.24.108. If you recall, we discussed how the DNS master registry system was established to link human-readable computer names to IP numeric addresses, basically like a digital "phone book."

This master registry system is overseen by ICANN (Internet Corporation for Assigned Names and Numbers), the organization that establishes administrative policies. This non-profit body also determines the TLD (Top Level Domain) names that you are familiar with, such as .com, .org and .edu, as well as less familiar ones such as .biz, .info and .mobi.

ICANN delegates the actual registration process to a group of accredited domain name registrars who maintain the actual registries, known as WHOIS. You are searching these registries when you are trying to get a domain name. If a domain has been registered to someone else, then there will be an entry in the WHOIS directory for that domain, so you can't register the same domain.

Network Solutions was the original registrar and had a monopoly. They charged $70 a domain for two-year registrations. This situation changed when ICANN allowed more registrars, who then actively competed for business, including buying and selling previously-registered names. There is even a small industry that specializes in providing a market to transact ownership of domain names, known as the domain aftermarket.

Prices dropped drastically with the increase in competition, so now annual fees are about $10 a year. This led to domain "cybersquatters" who registered thousands of domain names to make a profit. Now it's common to immediately reserve a domain if there is any possibility of needing it. Then you can sell the domain name or allow it to expire.

Domain names can have substantial business value. Domains such as movies.com and books.com are highly valuable properties. Early entrepreneurs locked up single word domains and then profited from selling domains for development as revenue-generating websites.

Companies quickly learned to register the domain names for their brands, and obvious extensions. Chagrined, they also moved to register negative domains. Target, for example, registered TargetSucks.com. They learned to keep track of their domain registrations and pay the annual fees. There have been some embarrassing goofs when fees weren't paid, and websites went down. Mighty Microsoft forgot to renew passport.com in 1999 and hotmail.co.uk in 2003.

Much like choosing your real estate agent, ask for recommendations when you are choosing a registrar. The ones I use are listed on the JustAskJean.com website. Service and user interface are the most important factors to consider, not the price. Registrar services are provided by these types of companies:

- Domain Registrars who are directly in the business of registering domain names. They may have links to other services, such as website hosting, but their primary business model is the annual revenue from domain owners.

- Resellers of domain names who get a commission from domain registrars. Essentially they are a marketing arm, and function in the same way that resellers of wireless services function. Their business comes from widespread advertising. Customer service can be poor or non-existent, since it may consist of only an email address, with email being answered in an unknown length of time. I ran into this problem when I was looking for an alternative to the expensive Network Solutions option, and paid for it in frustration.

- Website hosting companies who register domain names on behalf of their customers, but whose primary business is providing disk space for websites as well as other software and technical services. Changing website hosting companies is common as websites grow and is relatively straightforward. Changing registrars, however, is a time-consuming hassle.

  A hosting company may provide a "free" domain name registration, but switching the registration itself to another hosting company can be expensive or well nigh impossible. Hosting companies are more likely to go out of business, or have service degradation, than registrars. (Only die-hard techies and businesses with an IT department attempt to host their own sites.)

Basic Business 101 will save big-time hassles. Look for a phone number and chat with customer service before doing any business with a company. Ask about transferring domains. Transferring in is usually easy and directions are available on the new registrar site as a Frequently Asked Question (FAQ). But how to's for transferring out to another registrar usually won't be documented.

My recommendation is to always, always, register domain names with an actual domain registrar or a highly reputable reseller who provides telephone support.

, LISTED AS OWNER OF THE DNS

Make sure you are listed as the owner of the domain name. Pay the registration fee directly, keep your email current and check ownership periodically. Unscrupulous companies have been known to hold websites hostage by retaining ownership of the domain, rather than transferring rights to the site owners as part of website development.

How Do I Register a Domain?

The actual registration process includes several steps that occur in not-so-obvious order, depending on the registrar:

- Creating an account for that registrar. This is the master account, and will include your login information and password. Be sure the email contact is a permanent email that you will be checking on a regular basis. I use my AOL account for this, since it is not affected by changing hosting or email services.

- Choosing the domain name. You will find a search box prominently displayed on the home page of any company that registers domain names. If you are registering a personal name domain, then you start immediately with this step, since the primary challenge will be finding out what is available by doing a search against the WHOIS registry discussed earlier.

  Otherwise, start this step with paper and pencil, and do some Google and Yahoo searching to see what websites have already been developed, and list potential domain names. Finding a good domain for your purposes will be a process of elimination during the actual search registration process, since many domain names are already taken.

- Establishing a legal owner, a billing contact and technical contact for each domain name: The registrar system was designed for web professionals (also known as webmasters) who work on multiple domains with multiple owners, so the infrastructure reflects that approach. Each domain has its own expiration date and contacts. I use my name for all three contacts, but you may hire a web professional to be the technical contact. You may have different technical contacts if you have multiple domains. Large organizations may have the legal department as the owner, and accounts payable as the billing contact.

- Selecting registrar services: Originally, most registrars had an all-inclusive fee for their services, and I still prefer that model since it doesn't require making any decisions. Most registrars have switched to an a la carte business model to generate additional revenue, now that the price of domains has plummeted.

The basic registration fee is reasonable. You will, however, be enticed with numerous additional services. Initially, you will need URL forwarding and email forwarding until you have a website hosting company. I generally ignore the various protection and privacy options, which you can explore later. *URL FORWARDING* *E-MAIL FORWARDING*

Do not sign up for website hosting services at this point. It's the equivalent of choosing your landlord before deciding on an apartment or a house. You'll make this decision later. Look carefully at all the checkboxes—buyer beware! Costs can escalate quickly at the individual domain level. Additional options can be added later—registrar relationships are usually long-term. *NO WEB HOSTING TO START*

Setting Up Your Domain

You can start using your new domain name as soon as you've paid the annual registration fee. Let's look at what you can implement immediately:

- Email forwarding to an existing email account (generally your ISP or web email account)

- URL forwarding to an existing web page

This forwarding approach is not technically elegant, but works well to get started. When you move up to a hosted website, the setup is different and will be covered in subsequent chapters.

After purchasing a domain name, set up email forwarding by locating the email forwarding option on your registrar's control panel. Then set up a record for each email you want to create.

Here's what I've done using www.Hover.com/jean, my current domain name registrar. I have created an email named jb@econtentstrategies.com which forwards to an email I use on a daily basis, newsforjean@gmail.com. The screenshot below shows you what I did to establish the email account. Additional email accounts can be added just as easily.

Then you can use URL forwarding to an existing web page you've created on someone else's computer. This usually has an undesirable URL, which can be hidden by using your own domain. Using my domain name registrar, Hover, I've set up this domain to forward www.jeanbedord.com to my LinkedIn profile web page, which is actually http://www.linkedin.com/in/jeanbedord. I can make changes at any time, since these are under my control, not the control of another organization. The screenshot below shows how I've accomplished this step.

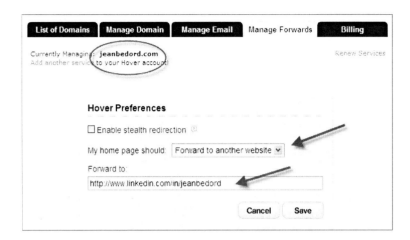

You can now put your personally branded domain, www.yourdomain.com on business cards. While I used LinkedIn as an example, you could also use Blogger.com (i.e. http://your blog.blogspot.com). I also used this technique with a family website at Comcast which includes limited hosting in their service. The actual website URL has the format http://home.comcast.net/~family/ where family@comcast.net is the corresponding email. This was impossible to explain over the phone to my non-technical uncle, given the location of "~" on the keyboard. So I used URL forwarding. Now he can type in an easy-to-remember family domain name, and even bookmark it in his web browser. I have the option of transferring the website to a more flexible hosting service, without even telling him about the move.

NOTE This setup may take 24 hours to propagate across the web to other computer servers. You do need to test forwarding and recheck it on a periodic basis, since your ISP may decide to block the forwarding.

Deciphering Name Servers

Now for an *oh-so-important* technical detail which is not intuitively obvious. The domain registrars are responsible for keeping the master WHOIS directories in sync with all the computers on the web. This is a monumental job which works amazing well. Each domain name needs to have an associated name server (computer), which maps ("resolves") the domain to its numeric IP address, such as 145.97.39.155.

When you register as domain name, your registrar will use their default name server codes in the DNS records. This is what my default registrar record looks like:

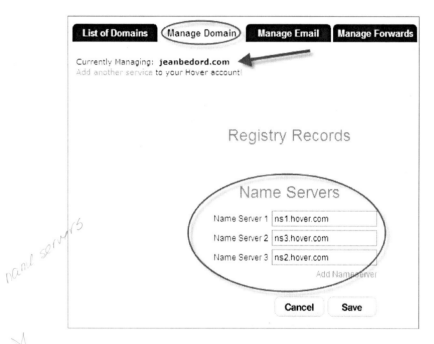

When you set up email forwarding and URL forwarding at your registrar, you are using their name servers.

You will need to change the name servers when you move up to a hosted website which has its own name servers. Your website hosting company will give you the addresses for their name servers (their computer addresses) when you set up the account. You will enter those addresses into the individual domain name record at your registrar (since you control access!). Then you will set up emails on your hosting computer service, just as you did at the registrar, as well as publish your website.

You can only have one set of name servers at a time! So you will either use your registrar or your web hosting service, but not both. Typically, you will develop your brand new website on a hosting service, test it, then change name servers when you want the new site to go public on the web.

This sounds more complex than it really is. Here's the screenshot of the setup for the name servers for my domain econtentstrategies.com, which is currently hosted at www.Bluehost.com/track/jbedord.

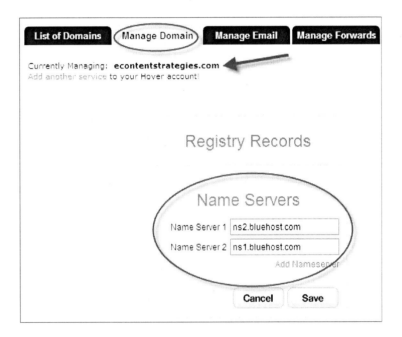

Managing Your Domain Names

Domains are valuable intellectual assets, but you won't spend much time on the registrar's website. I print out the pages for the account registration and profile, put it in a page protector, and put it in a 3-ring binder, labeled "Important Technical Stuff." Then I print out all my current registered domain names whenever another one is added, and put that in the same binder.

Automatic Renewal of your DNS

Opt for the automatic renewal when registering domain names, so valuable domain names are not lost. You can always opt out of automatic renewal to let a name expire. Be aware that some registrars charge credit cards automatically 30 to 45 days before the registration expires. There are no refunds.

As you register additional domains, each one will have a separate renewal date. Renewal notices are sent electronically to the email of record in the account—no hard copy, so keep your billing email current! Some registrars have syncing options so that all domains renew on the same date, which may be useful for a large number of domains.

If you are consolidating registrars or if you buy or sell domain names, be aware that transferring domain names to another registrar takes 30 to 60 days, so do this well before the expiration date for your domain. Transferring ownership of a domain name to a new owner and the registration at the same registrar is much simpler.

At this point, you have simply purchased the rights to an electronic address, and claimed your domain by adding email and URL forwarding. Now for the work of developing your virtual real estate....

USE EMAILS FOR DNS

aol
gmail

TRANSFERRING DOMAIN NAMES
• 30 – 60 DAYS
• CHECK W/ REGISTRA ON GUIDELINES
FOR TRANSFERRING

3 Using Your Domain Name for Email

How do I Set Up Email for my Domain?

Controlling delivery of your email is a major benefit of having your own domain name. Configuring your email is much like configuring your personal telephone services. You don't have to deal with either one at work since your information technology (IT) group sets up your phone and email. They negotiate with vendors on pricing and features. IT then makes the decisions on setup and configuration for the organization as a whole, not for you as an individual.

You have to make the same type of decisions that an IT department makes to set up email on your own domain, just with a different set of software and services. Mail, whether snail mail or electronic mail, is more complex than it appears on the surface. Let's look more closely at what's involved:

- Sending mail can be done anywhere. You can send snail mail from any place that has a postal pickup. Electronic mail can be sent from any computer with internet access. On an everyday basis, direct marketing companies use this capability to send advertising to both your snail mail and email boxes.

- Receiving mail requires an address which can be used by whoever is sending mail. You have to check your mailbox to actually get the mail. A snail mailbox can be at your home, your office, a post office or by general delivery. You have to "pick up" email by logging on to one or more mail accounts.

- Archiving snail mail is not a process I usually think about. Junk mail goes to the trash, bills go to the to-be-paid folder, and correspondence to other physical folders. Electronic mail archiving has different options. These include your personal computer desktop, your internet service provider (ISP), a mail server at a web hosting service, or web-based email (like Hotmail or Yahoo mail or Google mail).

A Closer Look at Archiving

Communicating with email involves all three of these intertwined processes. Let's start with the knottiest one—archiving, which takes the same thoughtfulness as storing all the "stuff" in a home.

Over the years, my archiving methods have changed with the technology. Initially, I kept electronic copies of messages in folders in the Outlook Express email program on my hard drive. This meant I had to start routinely backing up my email folders to recover from a hard drive crash (Yes, I had a crash and lost mail!).

The single hard drive approach had its limitations when I started using a laptop computer in addition to my desktop. On the road, I used the web-based email services provided by both my ISP and my website hosting service to keep my email on their services. Then I downloaded the email to my desktop computer when I got home. This worked to keep my email in sync, though I had to log on to each one separately and found their email interfaces less flexible than my desktop email.

I switched to web-based email services that can be accessed from any computer when Yahoo, and then Google, introduced essentially unlimited virtual space for archived email. Using Google email service has changed my habits, for better or worse, since I don't have to be as careful about cleaning up old email. Even more importantly, the search engine email services provide improved search, tagging and filtering capabilities.

Today, I rely heavily on my searchable archive of electronic mail. I'm not paranoid about storing my archive on Google Gmail, since it offers easy web access, tagging, filtering and search. Advertising is a minor annoyance, since print publications also have advertising. This, however, means managing my email files more carefully as assets—the type of function assumed by an IT department in an organization.

Places to Store Your Email

When using your own domain for email, you need to decide where the archive will be located, and address backups. If you are working for an organization, check out the frequency of the backups and email retention policies! Let's explore the implications of different options:

The hard drive on our own personal computer is the default archive for most of us. This, however, risks losing mail history with a hard disk drive crash. So regular backups of your email file (daily for heavy use) are essential. Backups can be to external media or you can pay for an automatic backup service (my preference, so I don't have to remember the daily chore).

Email can also be stored on an external computer server. It's common to use email services to store email at your web hosting company. You will need to manage the size of the email inbox, due to space limitations (same problem as office or university disk space). This works well for organizations with several employees so only the single server has to be backed up, instead of multiple workstations. Another location is your ISP, but my experience with Comcast is that their email management services are primitive. Broadband service providers are in the business of providing physical access and communication services, so email services are minimal.

STOREING E-MAIL OPTIONS
. STOREING E-MAIL @ THE WEB HOSTING CO.
. " " " YOUR ISP
. " " " WEB BASED SERVICES.

The latest option is storing email is web-based services, specifically Yahoo and Google, with their virtually unlimited storage area. (I've not exceeded 10% of my allocation.) I've gradually moved to relying more heavily on my searchable Gmail archive, but my older email is on my personal hard drive. And each one has to be managed separately!

Picking up Email

You receive email by logging into your email account(s) and using an email reader. Think of the email reader as the postman who collects emails from each computer server that is receiving email on your behalf, and putting it into your inbox.

While this sounds obvious, consistently receiving email requires building the habit of checking email accounts. Several years ago, I found some of my Little League baseball parents didn't always check their emails for schedule updates, so I had to follow up with reminder phone calls. Even today, some of my extended family members either check email just occasionally or have no email addresses at all.

Chances are you already have more than one email account that needs to be checked. Domain-based email means even more accounts, since it's easy to set up special purpose emails. Let's start counting email accounts:

- The first server that collects email is your internet service provider (ISP). If you are already getting email from your ISP, then your email reader has been correctly set up for that server. Information on how to set up (configure) your email is provided in the Frequently Asked Questions (FAQs) on their website. My ISP is Comcast, so I have an email account with them that looks like mylogon@comcast.net.

- Your website hosting company is the server that collects email for any email addresses you've set up for your website. You can choose to use their mail services for the archive or forward your emails to your ISP or web email account. My website is set up with Jean@econtentstrategies.com and JB@econtentstrategies.com which is forwarded to my Gmail account for spam control.

- Your domain registrar is another server that receives email and forwards to another account. I use this name server for my Jean-Bedord.com domain, which doesn't have its own website but does have email forwarding for jb@jeanbedord.com.

- If you set up a Google, Yahoo or Hotmail email account, these are more in-the-computing-cloud servers receiving email in your account(s). I have a Yahoo account to use Yahoo Groups and a Google account for my main email.

Checking these individual accounts on a regular basis is tedious, so you use an email reader to check all of them at the same time. There are two basic approaches:

- Personal computer email readers

- Browser email services

A personal computer email reader (also called a client) is the software most of us used to learn to use email. The program is installed on our hard drives, and creates an archive there. Microsoft Outlook is the typical corporate email reader, which works with Microsoft Exchange server.

I prefer to use its simpler cousin, Outlook Express, which has been replaced by Windows Mail or Windows Live Mail in the newer Microsoft releases. Mozilla Thunderbird is one of many open source email programs that work on several operating systems. Depending on the reader, you can set up the reader to collect the mail automatically every time you open the program, by setting up a schedule to send and receive, or manually, by clicking Send/Receive on the reader toolbar.

So how does the email get from the server to your email reader? Setup details depend on the software you are using as well as the server. Start by getting the documentation from each of the servers that will be sending you mail. There will be information about configuring various email clients somewhere under technical support or within the knowledge base.

Now you open your email program, and go looking under the tabs for Accounts (meaning email accounts), Options, or Tools. You will need to enter information about each one of the email accounts which are to be picked up and delivered to your personal computer. I have to enter both JB@econtentstrategies.com and Jean@econtentstrategies.com, since these are two different accounts on my website hosting service. Both accounts have the same information about the server, which is:

1. Incoming and outgoing mail server identifiers and

2. Account information to sign in on your behalf and collect the email. This is the same as receiving mail under different names (for example, maiden vs. married names) in the same snail mail-box.

The email software on your personal computer fetches your mail and pulls it down to your hard drive. This lets you then log off from the internet connection to read and write your email. This was the standard approach before high-speed internet access became common and is still quite useful if you are on the road, rather than at a desk.

With the advent of high-speed internet access, web-based email services (Hotmail, Yahoo Mail, and then Gmail) were created. These browser-based email services have become popular. You may not think of them as email readers, but they also let you send and receive email.

Web-based email services function differently from the desktop email reader. You set up your email accounts on the different mail servers to automatically forward all incoming emails to your web email account. This means that email is received continuously, rather than having the email client periodically poll all your email servers. This approach works best if you are constantly on a high-speed internet connection.

Synchronizing Devices

Now let's explore the complexities of multiple computers. Traditional email readers originated with desktop computers. You had one computer, and email was downloaded to the inbox on your hard drive. There was only one archive to manage.

Then one day, you started using other computers, with a laptop for travel, but continued to use the desktop as your primary computer and kept your email archive on that computer. Checking email on the road could be done by checking individual email accounts using web mail (for example, http://mailcenter.comcast.net or http://yourdomain.com/webmail). This is cumbersome for multiple email accounts, though it is still the only alternative when utilizing public access computers in libraries, conferences and internet cafes.

You have an alternative with your own mobile computer to set up the email reader exactly the same way it is configured on the primary computer, email account by email account, including server addresses. However, this means that new email is delivered to that computer, rather than to the primary computer. There is an option, however, to keep copies of the messages on the server, in addition to the copy that is downloaded. When you return to your home or office, the copies of messages received on your mobile computer can also be delivered to your primary computer and/or can be maintained on the server.

Now for the synchronization problem. Traditional email delivery is based on POP (Post Office Protocol), which means that delivery is one way down to your computer. Reading your email is not a problem, but other actions don't get communicated back to your server or your primary computer. Replies and deletions are specific to the computer that you are using, so keeping your files in sync is tedious. There is a second protocol called IMAP (Internet Message Access Protocol), which permits two-way communication between your computers and the server. This means that it's easier to keep email deletions and replies in sync.

Sound confusing? It is. Availability of IMAP, which is the recommended protocol, is dependent on the service you are using. You will find this information in the setup documentation. Then you'll need to experiment and test different settings to find the optimal configuration for your situation. Some of your services may support IMAP, and others may support only POP.

Since I have chosen to use Gmail as my email archive, I want copies to stay on the server, but I can also choose to download the email to the email reader on my hard drive. Here's what the setup screen looks like to make those choices:

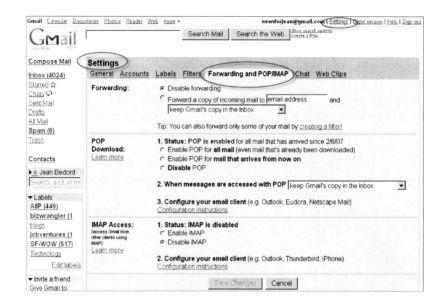

Spam Control

Now for another major consideration. We all have to deal with an inordinate amount of email spam. Your ISP and website hosting services have some type of spam filter. The spam ends up in one of two places: to your email reader if you forward all your email, or into a spam folder on your server account. No spam filter is perfect, so individual spam folders need to be reviewed, but sorting through spam ranks low on my priority list.

So, I've resorted to using web-based email instead. Google, Yahoo and Hotmail have many more resources for fighting spam than my other service providers. I forward all email accounts to my web-based email (gmail.com) for spam filtering. I only have to review one spam folder, rather than individual account folders.

I use my Google Gmail filters to label (tag) each email by domain, i.e. any email addressed to Jean@econtentstrategies.com has an EContent label, any email addressed to my San Jose State University email Jean.Bedord@sjsu.edu has a SJSU label. This gives me a unified inbox, but with labels to easily identify the different email sources.

This approach, as well as the decision to keep my archive on the web, has changed my habits. Now I review my email initially on Gmail—much like sorting the mail from my snail mail box, deleting as much as possible. As I read the email, I can add additional tags by subject, so an individual email can have multiple categories. Then I can download the important email to my personal computer, while keeping a copy on Gmail. Here's a screenshot that shows my inbox. An email is found in only one folder, but can have multiple labels.

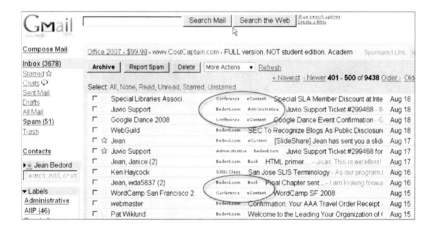

Sending Email with Your Domain

Just like sending a snail mail postcard, sending an email can be done from any computer, anywhere in the world, as long as the sender has a TO address. The electronic equivalent of a postal office mark is the FROM address on the email showing the origin of that email. The journey around the web is documented in the cryptic codes buried in the email header.

Your email reader is used to send as well as receive email. Your email reader can send out emails under different email accounts, just as it can receive mail from multiple accounts. It's the equivalent of using the same mailbox on your porch to send snail mail to different members of your family.

When you set up your software to receive emails from multiple servers, you specified individual email accounts. These included the accounts you set up for your domain. Any of these addresses can be used as the FROM address when you are composing or replying to another email. Look for a drop-down box on the FROM line, and pick the one you want to use.

My default FROM entry is the Comcast account, myaccount@comcast.net, but I don't use that for correspondence since it is ISP specific, not my domain address. From the drop-down box on the FROM line, I can choose from Jean@econtentstrategies.com or Jean@Bedord.com or Jean.Bedord@sjsu.edu depending on my role when writing the email.

NOTE IT controlled email probably won't have this option—you have one identity such as employeeX@yourcompany.com.

Web-based email can be used the same way, with details varying by service. My Gmail account allows me to send FROM different email addresses, so I never use the address myaccount@gmail.com for either sending or receiving email. Unlike my desktop email reader, Gmail requires verification that I control the email address, a simple automated process. These are the email accounts that I've set up for Gmail:

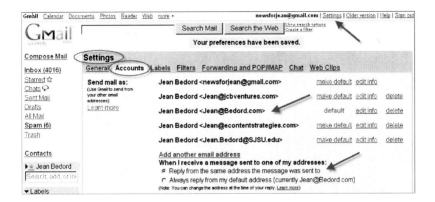

Any of these emails can be used to send email FROM my Gmail account:

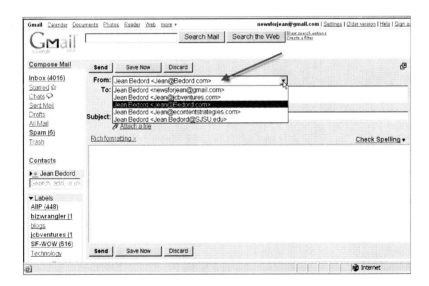

Optimizing your Domain Email

There isn't a one-size-fits-all best solution for managing email for your domain. The only way to figure out what works for you is to experiment with different combinations. Then test, test, test by sending and receiving emails from your domain email, using different combinations.

Sign up for an account at one of the web-based email providers and try sending and receiving email messages to see if you like the interface. Then try sending and receiving from that service as well as downloading to your hard drive.

Change the default email in your reader to your new domain email. Look closely at options inside each component, and keep track of where each test message ends up.

Not to be overlooked; keep notes on your testing. Take screenshots to include in your documentation, in case you need to reconstruct your settings. You'll want to make changes at some point, and your notes will help reconstruct your thought processes and decisions. You'll also need them for configuring other changes to your computing world:

- Additional domains

- Additional email services

- New computers and mobile devices, such as smart phones

Domain-based email improves contact management, but it does force decisions about other aspects of email management. Now on to more web technology!

4 Using Your Domain Name for a Website

What Type of Website Should I Develop?

Just as most of us started our home ownership lives with starter homes, websites can be developed in phases, remodeling or moving up as needs change. Surfing the web and looking at similar websites is the equivalent of a real estate tour. If you were buying a home, a tour is a good way to decide what type of home you would like to buy, whether condominium, townhouse, single family home or Victorian historical house. Just like houses, there are tradeoffs and costs associated with different website choices.

Start your website tour by going to Google or to your favorite search engine and putting in some search terms related to your website. Look at the different websites that come up, and identify what you like and don't like about each one, noting the URLs for later reference (Does this sound like research?). If you are familiar with a website that is similar to the one you will be building, take a closer look at its look and feel. Look at how many pages are included in the website and the linking structure between the web pages.

The sheer number of choices can be overwhelming, much like looking for a place to live. There are, however, some basic types of websites to consider, ranging from free to custom design. So let's take a closer look at some different options.

Option: Public Profiles

You may already have a public profile available on another organization's website. You may not have considered this option for a website, but for a basic resume or one page informational site, a profile is a workable option.

Social networking sites such as MySpace, Facebook and LinkedIn have become quite popular on the web. As a member of a community, you build an editable profile, which is essentially a personal web page. Each social networking site has its own demographics, with friends using the same site.

LinkedIn is particularly useful for business professionals and provides for a public profile in addition to the more extensive private profile available to other members of your network. The public information is indexed in the search engines, which makes your profile findable. MySpace also allows you to have a public web page, a feature heavily used by alternative music groups and other organizations. Individuals can also have public web pages on MySpace, but they have a different look and feel than LinkedIn. Facebook profiles are not as publicly visible at this point, but this can change. There are other social networking sites, particularly internationally.

As described in Chapter 2, I use URL forwarding at my registrar so my domain www.jeanbedord.com displays my LinkedIn profile. However, before taking that step, I edited my profile inside LinkedIn to convert the default URL from this gibberish http://www.linkedin.com/pub/0/662/0b1 to http://www.linkedin.com/in/jeanbedord which makes more sense in both URL forwarding and search engine results.

I also teach part-time at San Jose State University, so I have a profile on their website at http://slisweb.sjsu.edu/people/faculty/bedordj/bedordj.php which is a rather convoluted URL. I could use this as an alternative URL for my jeanbedord.com domain.

Squidoo is another website that allows community members to build public web pages based around subject knowledge. Your ISP may include a site builder template and website hosting in their services. AOL offered an early version of this at http://hometown.aol.com which still available but no longer promoted. And there are other alternatives.

The advantage to these profiles is that they are free and relatively easy to build using templates. No knowledge of HTML is needed, and you don't need a web host. The downside is that there is little flexibility—either they meet your needs for a website or you should look for alternatives. The other major disadvantage is that the primary URL structure is their domain, so you need to use URL forwarding at your domain registrar to make your web page findable under your own domain.

Option: Blogs as Websites

Blogging websites can be an attractive alternative if you want to have a website that has more than one page. Ignoring the media hoopla about citizen journalism and the blogosphere, blog technology is quite useful in building websites that need to be kept up to date, particularly by non-technical people. You can build a blog site without a web hosting service, whereas updating traditional websites requires some technical knowledge to interact with the web hosting service.

The software to set up blogs has become much more flexible than when blogs were first introduced. The blog website structure consists of static pages and postings. One of the static pages may be labeled About Me or Contact, which can be the equivalent of a personal web page. These static pages can have other labels, depending on the purpose of the website, and basically consist of information that doesn't change frequently.

New information is added by posting an entry, which is essentially sending an email message to the website. Postings are generally described as journal format, which means each one is relatively short, with a time and date stamp, typically displayed in chronological order, with the most recent entry first. Postings may also be categorized into subject areas to make finding older posts easier.

Libraries were early adopters of this technology, so library aides could post current events without having to get scarce programming support. They quickly adopted a multiple blog strategy, with one blog for events and another for recommended books. They also developed how-to-blogs, with links back to the main website.

Simple blogs are relatively easy to set up, and are based on drag-and-drop templates. Changing the formatting of all the blog web pages can be done simply by changing the template (also called a theme). It's the ease of changing the look and feel of the entire website that causes blog software to be called an inexpensive Content Management System (CMS).

The choices for blogging software have narrowed to three major contenders, each with different tradeoffs.

Google's Hosted Blogger Service

Blogger.com is the original blogging software company. It was bought by Google, and is provided as a free service. The price is right and you don't have to choose a web hosting company. The downside is the lack of customer support. There are extensive public forums and how-to articles, but no friendly customer support telephone service.

Blogger actually comes in two flavors. The more common flavor is the hosted version with a URL that looks like http://blogspot. yourblog.com. You can use URL forwarding to forward your domain name to the Blogger URL, but the individual entries will have the blogspot URL. If you ever decide to change blogging platforms, and other websites link to your individual posts, those links will disappear.

Blogger in this hosted form works well for personal websites. I have a nephew who chronicled his volunteer work in Sri Lanka after the tsunami using Blogger—it was his way of communicating with the family when he had to rely on internet cafes. I have a family blog and use URL forwarding so my eighty-year-old aunt can remember the domain name.

The URL problem can be solved by using Blogger as a publishing platform on your own web hosting service, but setting it up is rather technical. It's an older approach that has been superceded by other technologies.

Six Apart's Typepad Hosted Service

This blogging service, www.typepad.com, is preferred by business professionals who want customer support, but don't want to deal with a web hosting service. Typepad charges a monthly fee, based on the number of blogs.

Just like domain names, it's easy to end up with multiple blogs! You may find yourself not just with a blog for your professional life, but with blogs for your personal and family life, with photo albums and podcasts. It's easy to allow multiple authors, so others can contribute to the website.

A key advantage of Typepad is that you can use your own domain name, instead of using URL forwarding to your domain, as necessitated by Blogger. This means that the permalinks (permanent links) to the individual postings will have your domain, not someone else's domain name in the URL.

Wordpress Software

Wordpress is an open source, meaning free, software that has become quite popular for blogging. The advantage of open source is the extensive volunteer developer community, which contributes new plug-ins and widgets to expand features. The downside is that you have to actively manage upgrades to the software and troubleshoot problems as they occur. It's a lot like managing Microsoft products on your own personal computer, with third party add-ons, which may or may not work with your current release.

Wordpress does require a website hosting service, and the software is frequently included in their services. The basics are easy to set up, but customizing takes some technical understanding. The good news is that there is a growing community of web professionals available for hire with Wordpress skills. Once the blog is set up, updating is as easy as any other blogging service.

Your domain name can be used for the URL of the blog, since the software resides on your account at the website hosting service. If your plans include other types of websites that require a web hosting service, then Wordpress is a choice to consider.

Wordpress is quite popular in universities for both students and faculty, as well as the technical community. There is also a free hosted version at www.wordpress.com, but the version does not have all the plug-ins and features of the open source software. And it, too, lacks customer support, other than the developer community.

I've used all of the blogging services, and just like any other tool, there are advantages and disadvantages to each one. The key differentiators are:

- Level of customer service—free means no commercial support

- URL structure management—complete control vs. URL forwarding

Overall, I've been amazed by the flexibility of blogging technology as a whole, with the ease of updating, and use of static vs. posting pages. But there are other types of websites to consider during your tour of the web....

Option: Websites on a Web Hosting Service

Traditional websites are hosted on a web hosting service with your domain name. A website consists of one or more web pages. Creating a website on your local computer, then publishing it to a web hosting service is a more flexible option than social networking profiles or blogging software, with more options to determine the look and feel.

Let's look at the types of websites you would develop on a website hosting service:

One Page Mini-sites

A one-page website is like a one-room home, so there are no hallways or other rooms. Size does not matter, since web pages are not constrained by print formats. A one-page mini-site can be as simple as a dry-cleaner with the business name, address, and phone number, a picture of the storefront and some type of advertising message. Or it can be the same information found on a business card, with room for some additional information. Converting existing print information to an HTML coded web page is straightforward.

Have you ever gotten a thirty-page sales letter in the mail from a direct marketer? Well, that becomes a single web page website that scrolls and scrolls. It can have pictures and video testimonials embedded in it.

Marketers frequently use one-page mini-sites for special offers. These are stand-alone pages with a single action item—this could be a giveaway with registration, a special price on a product, or a printable coupon.

Real estate professionals often create a mini-site for each of their properties, using the property name as the domain name, with pictures and even a virtual tour of the property. These are relatively inexpensive to create compared to print collateral, and can be removed when the property is no longer on the market.

Creating a one-page website is much like creating a single document in a word-processing program such as Word. You can save a Word document in HTML format, and use this as a one-page website. However, print formatting is inherently different from web formatting, so the results may not be attractive.

Web pages are best created using a different set of tools, which are covered later in this book. If you already have a brochure or marketing collateral in print format, it's relatively easy to convert this to a simple HTML website since the words and images (copy) for the web page already exist.

Portfolio Multi-page Informational Websites

Just as a home with multiple rooms requires doorways, a website with multiple pages requires links, also called hypertext links, to navigate from page to page. Just as each room has a specific function, each web page needs to have a purpose.

My consulting website, www.econtentstrategies.com, is a portfolio website. The front door is the main page, also called a home page or an index page, which has links to other pages in the website. The Home page conveys the purpose of the website, with links to additional web pages for Services, Writing, Speaking, Press and About, the last of which displays a bio. This is similar to many other consultant websites. The purpose is informational, and it's essentially an online equivalent of a promotional kit.

Graphic artists, photographers and other artists typically build portfolio sites. My library school students at San Jose State University complete their MLIS degree by building a portfolio site to show their academic work and credentials. It's a great way for employers to evaluate potential employees or contractors.

Service businesses frequently build this type of website when they've outgrown their one-page website. Professional services, in particular, may want to post resources for their clients on a website, rather than mailing out forms. Accountants will have links to forms on the IRS site, as well as explanations of which forms clients will need depending on their business.

The complexity of this type of website varies directly with the number of web pages, with navigation becoming a key element of the design and usability. The web pages themselves can range from simple to complex, with links to other services, such as an email signup.

Option: Industry-Specific Template Sites

Many websites are built from templates. Professional practices, in particular, can have comparable website structures. Dentists all provide similar services, as do CPAs. Starting with a template reduces development costs, while the overall look and feel can be customized.

A key consideration is whether you can use your own domain for the URL. Sometimes, these template sites provide a subdomain on their primary domain, so you have to use URL forwarding.

For example, my accountant has the domain name mcl-cpa.com, which he uses on his business cards and materials. However, when I enter www.mcl-cpa.com, this immediately forwards, and the final URL in the browser is https://www.webbuildersolution.com/websites/33397/index.htm. His domain and name are not in the URL, a key factor for the search engines.

If he were using a service with a mappable domain, then the URL would be www.mcl-cap.com/contact for his contact page instead of https://www.webbuildersolution.com/websites/33397/2.htm (The last fragment, 2.htm indicates that this URL points to page 2 of the website, a poor structure for search findability).

NOTE This structure is common in older web builder services.

An additional downside is that these industry templates may not necessarily fit your business. My brother sells farm and ranch real estate. His clients care about the type of property for sale, whether it's irrigated or dryland, a horse training property, or a cow-and-calf operation. His not-so-great websites (three so far) have been based on templates appropriate for searching for residential real estate where town location is important, as well as the number of bedrooms in the house. (For the type of properties he represents, the house is incidental!)

Option: Websites Selling Affiliate Products/Services

Selling products and services on the web requires a different type of website, which can be single or multiple pages. The objective is to actually make a sale, and make money, rather than just provide information.

The simplest form of selling is through commissioned sales of products which are produced by other people, called affiliate links in the web world. This form of selling means someone else manages the inventory, fulfillment, and collecting money, while you get a commission for the sale.

While there are affiliate marketing experts who make a living from these commissioned sales, this type of website is quite useful for market research and prototyping. Web traffic and sales conversion, called landing page conversion, is critical to any web business.

Starting a business by developing a website with affiliate links to other people's products to determine demand and build web traffic is a low-cost, low-risk way to enter markets. Bootstrap website development allows for the inevitable delays in developing a substantial business, with minimal fixed overhead costs. There are learning curves for all of this technology, and deferring the costs, time, and energy of product development improves the chances of success.

Let's look at some scenarios:

- I want to set up a new business that specializes in eco-friendly knitting yarns. By building a website using affiliate programs, and doing some offline and online advertising, I can determine level of interest and what types of products sell. Some products don't sell, either in bricks-and-mortar or online, so I can determine winners before investing in inventory. Furthermore, a successful proof of concept with the website will be more persuasive with my banker, if I need a loan to scale up the business.

- I'm interested in developing a sideline business to supplement my current income, in case I lose my job. Over the years, I've tried a number of diet programs, and have found some were more successful than others. So I develop a website with reviews of different diets, with tips on how to select one that is best for your personal life style.

- As a consultant, I've evaluated and selected a number of products and services that I use in my day-to-day practice. Many of these have affiliate programs. So I've developed a website, www.JustAskJean.com, with those recommendations.

I've known too many entrepreneurs who spent months, even years, filing patents and developing products, only to discover there was limited market demand. Identifying the target market, and finding out what people will actually buy, provides the groundwork for product development. Much like a phased home remodel, building a website and marketing strategy based on a plan for additional product development makes the business launch process more doable. Extensively revamping a website is much less expensive than modifying a patented product because customers don't like it.

Many, many companies have affiliate programs. The key to success in affiliate marketing is to start with one or two programs and a limited number of products for a target market. Specialized (niche) markets are easier to reach, and perform better in the web world.

You will need to qualify each of the programs and products, since you don't get paid unless the merchant actually fulfills the sale satisfactorily. Some of the major players are:

Amazon.com for Physical Products

Amazon is the granddaddy of affiliate programs on the web. It's still one of the largest, particularly for books. Our students in the distance education program are asked to purchase their textbooks through an affiliate link for the San Jose State University library school. This successfully generates money for graduate school scholarships.

Amazon has a wide variety of products, good product fulfillment and customer service. As a business, you are freed up to do the marketing and drive web traffic.

ClickBank for Digital Products

ClickBank is another pioneer in affiliate marketing. It has a variety of digital products, specifically downloadable ebooks and software. ClickBank is essentially a marketplace broker for these products, so you are dependent on each individual merchant to fulfill the sale. Steps for completing the sale are not standard, since these are individual businesses.

Commission Junction for Variety

Commission Junction was so successful that it has been acquired by Value Click, a leader in web advertising. Merchants are called publishers, meaning they have websites that sell products and services. It, too, is a broker providing administrative services to connect buyers and sellers.

Affiliate commissions vary widely depending on the product. Commissions are low on physical products, and Amazon's are among the lowest. Digital products have the highest commissions, since fulfillment costs are low. Lead generation commissions can be substantial, since other means of lead generation, using traditional marketing, can be quite expensive.

Option: E-Commerce Websites

From a marketing standpoint, affiliate sites and e-commerce sites are quite similar. E-commerce sites, however, take payments and provide fulfillment. This process is much easier for an existing business that already has a merchant account and credit card processing in place, since they can be used for both the web and bricks-and-mortar transactions. Plus, an existing business already has already developed the business expertise, and is typically looking to expand their marketing channels.

My favorite example is www.swivel-chair-parts.com which has replacement parts for tilting and swivel chair parts, both office and home. The walk-in repair service is Abacus in Houston, Texas, but they have leveraged their knowledge and parts inventory to provide a service not available at furniture or office stores. I appreciated the detailed specifications in trying to figure out the right replacement part. Plus they have tips on installation so we can do it ourselves.

This is an example of a customized website tailored to the needs of an existing business, specifically the plethora of different replacement parts, so it is a fairly large website. New businesses starting on the web can start with a template website, and then move to a customized version, as the business develops.

There are two basic approaches to collecting money with e-commerce sites:

PayPal and Google Checkout

These are the simplest systems to implement and are suitable for low-volume transactions, particularly for services. Paypal is basically a payment system that grew up with online auctions to provide a means of payment for people who didn't have credit cards. It has expanded to handle multiple currencies, which can be quite useful. I used Paypal to send donations to my nephew in Sri Lanka, and he could get rupees at the local bank. Another common use is registering and collecting money for events, since there are no monthly minimums required, just a transaction fee. Google Checkout is a newcomer, and more useful in the context of other Google products.

Shopping Cart Software

Amazon pioneered this technology, and it has become ubiquitous in web technologies. You would choose this type for selling physical products since it integrates with ordering and inventory software. There are multiple versions, ranging from standalone software to embedded versions included in industry-specific site builder services.

Implementing a shopping cart does require more expertise than other types of websites. Product fulfillment process includes pricing and sales taxes, which need to be paid and reported, as well as online receipts. A merchant account and credit card processing are required, and those do involve minimum monthly payments.

Now that you've taken a tour of different types of websites, you've probably decided on what you want for your starter website. So now let's dig into some of the *oh-so-important* technical details that make a difference.

5 Learning the Jargon

What's the Difference Between a Website and a Web Page?

Understanding the terminology is one of the major challenges in utilizing web technologies. Let's start with basics. A website (also spelled web site with a space), also known as a site, is a collection of one or more web pages. A personal website might be a single web page, but a business website could be thousands of individual web pages.

Web pages are similar to pages in a document, with some major differences. Word processing formatting is designed for hard copy. The codes are invisible to the author, but are passed to the printer software drivers to create attractive output. These codes, originally designed for typesetting, aren't compatible with documents designed to be web pages.

Documents designed as web pages are coded using Hyper Text Markup Language, known as HTML. Instead of cryptic codes, this language uses text tags such as <title> and <p> to format the ASCII text. These pages look quite unintelligible until they are opened in a web browser, such as Microsoft Internet Explorer (IE) or Mozilla Firefox or the new Chrome from Google.

Web pages are designed to be viewed on a computer screen, not as printouts. The HTML tags make the web page readable, setting the font size and style, placement of the pictures on the page, and the overall look and feel.

Just as a long Word document will have a table of contents, a website has a navigation scheme with links among the pages. It's the same concept as creating multiple pages in a Microsoft Word document, but instead of turning the pages, there are HTML links to move from web page to web page.

The process of developing content for either the print world or the online world is very similar—the hard work is in developing the concept, the images and the words (copy) to convey the message of your website. The difference is the tools used for implementation.

Planning Your Website

Just as you learned to develop presentations in PowerPoint or documents in Word, there are two parts to your website creation project:

- Creating the content of the website—the information that is being conveyed. You provide the expertise for this aspect.

- Utilizing tools to complete the website—and there are learning curves associated with each tool, so the key is picking the right one for each particular project.

The best way to start a website project is the old-fashioned way, with a pencil and large index cards. Each card represents a web page. The first one is the Home page which should clearly convey the purpose of the website. Another card is the About page, with your bio and contact information. There could also be a card labeled Writing, for the articles and books you've written. Another card can be Services, and then additional cards with details on each product.

This exercise will tell you the size of your website project. A single page website is much easier to implement than one with 5–10 web pages, which in turn is easier than a 100-page website. Size of the project is a major factor whether you do it yourself or hire a web professional.

The second major factor is the nature of the content, which will determine the architecture of your website. A one-page contact site can be implemented using a social media profile or a mini-site with a website host. A one-page sales letter will be a mini-site on a website host. A professional practice with static information will be a multi-page website on a website host. A portfolio website will be a blog or a multi-page website.

Software Tools You'll Need

Word-processing programs such as Microsoft Word are standard in the print world. You can actually save a Word document in HTML format, and use this as a one-page website. However, print formatting is inherently different from web formatting, so the results may not be attractive.

Web pages are best created using a different set of tools:

- A simple, all-purpose text editor, which you've probably used in other applications.

- An HTML editor.

If you are using a computer running Windows, a basic text editor, Notepad, is available by navigating, from your Start menu, to Programs > Accessories. Text editors were designed for programmers writing software code, with no frills like fancy formatting or spellcheck. I prefer a different text editor, TextPad, which includes a spellchecker (See JustAskJean.com for details).

Text editors are key tools to converting word-processing documents to HTML web pages. They remove the printer codes from the document and change the words to plain unformatted text, which can then be copied into an HTML editor for web page formatting.

A text editor can be used to create web pages, but you need to manually code in the HTML tags for fields and formatting, such as <b> for bold and <p> for paragraph. This is quite tedious for anything more than a plain page. You then have to open the file in a web browser (Internet Explorer or Firefox or other) to view the actual appearance. Needless to say, there are no diagnostics when your web page looks strange!

HTML editors are the web equivalent of word processing editors. All HTML editors produce similar code. Ease of use is a key factor, and the newer HTML editors have visual editors which allow you to see what you are creating on the page. The actual HTML code is hidden until you switch to the Source view. You don't have to learn HTML, though it's easier to troubleshoot if you know the basics and can understand the code that is being automatically generated.

- FrontPage from Microsoft was one of the first HTML editors, and was included in the original Microsoft Office suite. It has fallen out of favor due to lack of development and kludgy code implementation. FrontPage has been superceded by Expression Web in the suite of 2007 products from Microsoft.

- Dreamweaver from Adobe is preferred by professionals, and has all the capabilities they need. It's probably overkill for most people, but has the advantage of widespread training and support. Just as we took classes to learn how to use Word, Excel and PowerPoint effectively, a class on using an HTML editor can be useful.

- NVU is the free open source software equivalent. This has a convoluted history originating with Netscape Composer, which became open source as part of Mozilla. One version was developed for Linux, which became NVU, which was also compatible with Macs and PCs. Newer upgrades are now named KompoZer. The obvious downside of NVU, as well as any free software program, is that support is limited to the community of developers.

- Other HTML editors are available—it's a matter of picking one that matches your budget and skillset. Regardless, utilizing web technologies means becoming comfortable with both text editing and HTML tools.

Developing the Website

You will be doing website development, meaning building your web pages, in one of two ways:

- Using software tools on your own computer (local) *or*

- Utilizing web page builders on a web hosting computer.

The difference is where you keep the working copy while developing the website.

In either case, you create and modify your web pages, before allowing access by others. Making your website accessible to the "public" is done by "publishing" the collection of web pages. Publishing is the very last step, the equivalent of the "ready for occupancy" stage in building a home.

Once you have the content written, with paper and pencil or in a text file, then you can start using tools to develop the actual web pages. This process is very similar to developing a PowerPoint presentation. You start by making some choices:

- Begin with a completely blank web page and build from scratch—the equivalent of a custom home. Graphic designers often make this choice, but I usually start with a template or model.

- Identify other web page designs you like and use them as models for building your own web pages. Much like decorating ideas during a real estate tour, you probably found design elements you liked or disliked when you were touring the web.

- Start with a template or previously developed web pages. Templates are readily available on the web or included in the commercial HTML editors. HTML templates are utilized much like templates for Microsoft Office products—they are simply preformatted pages that can be edited for your needs.

- Use a website builder to build the pages, either locally or on a website hosting site. Microsoft Publisher is an example of a software program that can build websites on your personal computer. Blogs, your LinkedIn profile and a Squidoo page are all examples of website builders. These are good as starter sites, since you can get a website up quickly using drag-and-drop design. The downside is that they lack flexibility, but the simplicity may be an acceptable tradeoff.

- Industry-specific site builders will build more complex sites quickly, and are generally hosted. These site builders can include e-commerce capabilities, which also reduces development time. One precaution is that these templates do not necessarily explain key fields clearly. My accountant's template website has a field called "Title," but there is no explanation that this is the metadata title for the web browser, not an on-page title.

As you build your website, it's good practice to stop and open your website with the major web browsers, Internet Explorer, Mozilla Firefox and Opera. HTML editors are not browsers, so your website may look different in a browser.

Website structure is different from Word documents and PowerPoint presentations, which consist of single files. Typically, you will have a folder of files for your website. The top level, the home page, will be named index.html. The other web pages will have names such as about.html which is the About web page, services.html which is the Services web page, and so on. There will also be images (.gif extensions) and pictures (.jpg extensions) for your web pages, as well as any PDFs that you are linking to on the website.

Much like any filing system, following good naming conventions will save headaches later. As websites grow, meaningful labels for individual web pages make sites much easier to maintain. If you have many images, add a folder labeled Images. My first website was built with Microsoft Publisher, which produced web pages named page1.html, page2.html, page3.html, etc.; hardly meaningful. This can be a problem with other website builders, since you don't control the URL structure.

When you've finished development, then it's time to make the website viewable on the web. This means "publishing" your website on the web. If you are using a site-builder website, then publishing may be as simple as clicking the Publish button, part of the simplicity of the site builder approach.

If you have created web pages on your local computer, then they have to be transferred to a hosting service. The publishing process requires some technical steps to make your website work—it's similar to getting a home computer network set up with routers. If you are doing it yourself, having telephone support from your web hosting service is crucial. You may want to consider hiring a web professional to complete this final step.

Now you have to have a computer to transfer this to—in computerese, a host server at a web hosting service.

Selecting a Website Hosting Service

You have many choices, perhaps overwhelming. If you happen to be part of an organization that allows you to put your personal web page on their site, you would follow their instructions on transferring the file. This is common in universities for faculty and staff. I have a faculty web page at San Jose State University http://slisweb.sjsu.edu/people/faculty/bedordj/bedordj.php. Notice, however, the URL won't fit on a business card, and the domain name is sjsu.edu, not my own domain name. Associations often provide the same service for their members, with the same problem.

Getting your own web hosting service provides the most flexibility. You are basically selecting a landlord for your website. Initially, you will share disk space with other website owners until your web traffic (and revenue) justifies a dedicated computer. Upgrading web hosting companies is common, particularly as the website develops from starter property to substantial revenue. The infrastructure needed to support a million dollar e-commerce site is different from that required for a personal or portfolio website.

Support is the key element for selecting a web hosting service. Starter packages for consumer level web hosting are inexpensive, and can start around $5–10 a month. Look for telephone service and actually call to test responsiveness and technical skill (both sales and technical support!) What hours is support available, business hours or 24/7? What level of uptime do they guarantee? If their computers are down, your website is not available on the web. Ask other website owners about their experiences—checking references is always good practice!

Pricing structure is a major issue, and the key is how the web hosting service charges for additional domains on their servers. There is a high probability you will have multiple domains, and multiple websites as you master web technology. Some of your websites may be single-page web pages; others may be portfolios or a blog. It's just much easier to have a single web hosting service, and learn their business practices.

So look for pricing that allows a number of domains for the same price, rather than pricing on a per-domain basis, which can add up quickly. I recommend a host with web-based cPanel (control panel) and Fantastico, which includes easy Wordpress blog installation, and other features. My current web hosting service is listed at JustAskJean.com.

If the technical details seem overwhelming in publishing your website, consider hiring a web professional. A webmaster does this technical work routinely, so can set it up so you can maintain the web page on an ongoing basis. I've hired a web professional to clean up my website code so that my site has a professional look.

Publishing Your Website

When you sign up for web hosting services, you will establish an account and password to administer your website, including the domain name to be hosted. You will receive an email with a number of technical details. Save both an electronic and paper copy of this important information. I print it out, put it in a document protector page, and keep it handy in my Important Technical Stuff binder. If you hire a web professional to help you with this step, they'll need to have the details in that email.

The publishing process includes several steps:

- Transfer your website file folder with the web pages, images, pictures, and documents that will be on your website to your domain name at the web hosting service. You will be using an FTP (File Transfer Protocol) process, either web-based on your host or a separate piece of software. A web-based version is simpler, particularly if your host has the Fantastico suite. Then test, test, test your website before going public.

- Set up your email accounts on your web host. If you have been using email forwarding or email servers at your domain registrar, they will be superceded by your web-host email. So you'll need to revisit your email configuration.

- Go to your domain registrar and enter the name servers for your hosting company into the registrar DNS name server records for your domain as described in Chapter 2.

NOTE The simplicity of changing the DNS name servers allow you to switch web hosting companies as websites grow or needs change. When I re-designed my website and changed web hosting companies, I made the name server changes at the registrar on Friday night, and the new address for the website was propagated across the Web by Monday morning.

Congratulations, your website can now be accessed on the world wide web...give yourself a big hug!

6 Making Your Website Findable in the Search Engines

How do I get Search Engine Visibility?

Congratulations, you've published your website and it can be viewed by other people. In the beginning, however, the only way they can find it is by knowing the exact URL. If you are building a website for your wedding or another personal event, then you'll send an email to your friends and family with the URL. For a portfolio website, you'll add it to your business card and resume.

Your website will not be findable (visible) in the search engines until their software crawlers discover the website and add it to their index files. It's like a telephone directory—your website has to be added before it can be found by searching. In my area, AT&T Yellow Pages and Valley Yellow Pages publish their print copies on different schedules, and include different businesses. Similarly, the search engines crawl the web on different schedules.

There is usually a delay before your website is crawled, which can be weeks or months. Crawling is done separately by each search engine, so your site can appear in Google,

Yahoo, Ask or any other search engine at different times. New domain names, and new websites, may not be allowed into the main index for a period of time to thwart creators of junk websites.

NOTE Changes to existing website pages are not immediately indexed, so the old web pages may remain in the search engine cache.

There are ways to help the search engine crawlers find your new website by getting it listed in other places. Some large megasites are crawled frequently, so mentions of your website provide links that the crawlers can follow to "discover" your website. The crawlers visit news websites particularly frequently, which is why a press release from PRWeb or PR Newswire will show up immediately in search results. Paid press release services are not new, but in the online world, they include embedded URLs in the release itself.

If you want visibility in the search engines, then plan on getting some initial links to your website. The links will depend on the type of website you have built and the purpose of the website. Putting your website URL (multiple URLs are allowed!) in your public LinkedIn profile is an easy way to provide a link for search crawlers to find your site. A Squidoo web page that you have built around a topic can provide yet another link. Other potential links depend on the purpose of your website.

Websites built with blog technology, either as standalone websites or as part of a larger static website, have an advantage in website visibility. The software can be configured to "notify" special-purpose ping servers when new posts are added to the blog. These ping servers are constantly visited by the search engines. This is the reason that breaking news frequently comes from blog sites updated by citizen journalists. Natural disasters such as floods and earthquakes can be reported within minutes using this type of technology.

This advantage is a reason to have a blog of some type included as part of a website. Evaluate the objectives for your site. Most of us will not be providing breaking news. Blogs can be used to provide thought leadership through your commentary on areas of your expertise. Commentaries do take time, though. Considering the time needed to provide fresh postings is part of deciding whether to select this type of website.

TIP A common website problem is having web pages that are not indexed for technical reasons. You can find out how many of your web pages are in a search engine index by going to Advanced Search, putting in your URL, and looking at the search results. You'll need to do some detective work to understand why any non-indexed pages aren't included in search results. And you may not want to have all web pages indexed. For example, you may choose not to index pages outlining your privacy policy or highlighting special, time-bound offers.

The screenshot below shows that 13 pages are indexed for my website www.econtentstrategies.com. I can compare that number to the number of pages on the site to see what has been indexed and what hasn't been indexed.

How do Searchers Find My Website?

Using the simple white search box pioneered by Google to find information in search engines has become part of our day-to-day activity.
But search is more complex than it looks on the surface, and making
your website findable to other people has several aspects. Inclusion in
the search engine indexes is just one building block.

People find information by using words in the search box, called a
search query (software engineers) or keywords (marketer) or search
terms (librarians). People are using words to describe what they are
looking for, not the URL of your website, so those words have to be
included in the copy (words) on your web pages. Images, pictures and
video without descriptions can't be indexed by today's technology, and
so can't be searched.

Though this seems obvious, your web pages must have words that can
be found and indexed by the search engines. Sometimes, a custom
website will have beautiful images and graphic design, but few words.
These websites may not be visible in the search engines, except by
specifying the URL or a direct link from another website.

Search technology is based primarily on keyword matches—the words
in the search query must closely match the words on the web page. As
the size of the web has grown and familiarity with search has increased, the number of words in the search query has increased. It's
pretty obvious that I will get different results if I search by "camera" vs.
"digital camera" vs. "digital camera review." Then if I specify "Nikon
digital camera," I'll bring up sites which are selling those cameras. De-
termining "intent" of the search query is part of the art of search!

Not everyone uses the same words to describe what they are looking
for, so it's important to use synonyms in the copy of your web pages.
Let's look at common situations:

- Misspellings are often handled by the search engines by providing
  alternative suggestions, with some interesting results. If I type
  "Bedord" (the correct spelling for my name) into Google, it says
  "Did you mean Bedford" (the misspelling of my name, yet a
  common surname). You don't need to have explicit misspellings in
  the copy for retrieval to work on close matches.

- Plurals are generally handled well by the public search engines, so that "goose" and "geese" are both retrieved. Incorporating both forms in your copy is a good practice since this means the copy is about the same subject.

- Spacing between words can be problematic. Sometimes, search results are different for "back pack" with a space and "backpack" without a space, a problem frequently found using search within the Yellow Pages. So both forms should be used in the copy on your web pages, even if your spellchecker objects!

- Acronyms should always be spelled out, and both forms should be used equally in the copy. The same acronym can have multiple meanings. For example, GPS can mean Global Positioning System or Gallons Per Second, depending on the context. Some acronyms and brand names, however, have crossed over into common usage. Who calls a DVD a "digital video disk" anymore?

- Alternative terms are poorly handled in the search engines. A search on "attorney" brings up different results than "lawyer," though we use the terms interchangeably. "Realtor" is a different search term than "real estate agent." This means that both termi-nologies need to be included in titles and web page copy.

- Expert language vs. lay language is a more subtle issue. A consumer is more likely to search by "cancer" but someone familiar with the medical literature may search by "oncology." The language on your website will depend on your intended audience, and how you want them to find it in the search engines.

Building web pages for your website is both an art and a science. Web pages have to carry a message for their intended audience, but the way in which they are constructed is also important. It's the difference between decorating your house and building the physical residence, both aspects of providing a comfortable home.

How do Searchers Find Answers?

You may think search is about finding your website, but search is about finding answers. The purpose of your website is the first question that needs to be answered, and this should be clear throughout the web pages on your site. The language you use in writing the copy is key, but there are some additional technical details that contribute to providing answers.

Let's look at the steps in a search:

I am looking for more information about a company named Third Door Media and their brands, so I enter the following search query, which retrieves a web page from Google, called a Search Engine Results Page (sometimes called a SERP).

Now let's look closely at the natural (or organic) listings in the center of the page. Here is one of them:

The **Third Door Media Brands**
Our **brands** and their upcoming search engine marketing webcasts, webinars and online events as well as conference events and expos.
thirddoormedia.com/**brands**.shtml - 7k - Cached - Similar pages
More results from thirddoormedia.com »

There will typically be ten entries like this on a search results page (this can be adjusted in the web browser settings). Let's look at where these components are generated and the corresponding HTML source code from the web page that has been retrieved:

- Title tag is the first line of the entry, and is the link to land on the corresponding web page, which may or may not be the home page for your site. Much like a newspaper or article, this is the most important element for the searcher, since they use this to decide whether to click through to your web page. After clicking through, the title shows up in the blue bar at the top of the browser, not on-page below the toolbar. A missing or poor title means no click-throughs. Every web page on your site needs a unique title. Notice the value of the information in the title—it is a close match to my search query.

- Description metadata provides a summary for the content on the web page. This is not always used by the search engines, but if there is no description, the search engines will algorithmically create a couple of lines. Better to have some control of what appears, rather than letting a computer decide. Each web page should have its own description; otherwise the pages can be treated as duplicate content. It's a common mistake to have the same description for all web pages in a website, since this may be the default for website builder software.

- Keywords metadata have mixed utility. Spammers have forced search engines to discount them, but I find them quite useful for documenting the keywords that are used for the copy on the web page, though the information is not displayed to the searcher (more on keywords later in this chapter). Websites in highly competitive niches don't want to document their keywords and will therefore omit this tag.

The URL for the web page is displayed on the last line. Your domain name is important to the relevancy of the search result snippet, and the decision to click through. In this case, the URL http://thirddoormedia.com/brands/ makes it clear that this page is about brands for this media company.

Below is the HTML source code from the web page. This information is not displayed below the toolbar in the web browser software, but the search engines find the code with their software crawlers and put it in their index files.

```
<head>

<title>The Third Door Media Brands</title>

<meta name="Description" content="Our brands and their
upcoming search engine marketing webcasts, webinars and online
events as well as conference events and expos." />

<meta name="Keywords" content="search engine marketing
events, search marketing conferences, search engine conferenc-
es, search marketing webcasts, online search marketing" />
```

Why are Keywords Important?

The words that a searcher enters into the search query box are commonly called keywords (or key words) by marketers. Analyzing what digital phrases are used and the number of people using them can improve the effectiveness of your online presence. Basically, you want the copy in your website to match the words that are actually being used online, not phrases that you are guessing that people use.

Let's look at how you can perform this analysis. Every time someone enters a series of words or clicks on a link, this is recorded for search engine analytics. This click stream data is humongous, so sampling techniques are used for analysis and relative measures. (It's this recording capability that concerns privacy advocates.)

The search engine companies analyze this data to manage their own infrastructure. Other companies purchase this information from the search engine companies, and then massage the raw data into mean-ingful results.

Keyword research is market research using this data from actual searchers to estimate markets and develop marketing messages. Compared to traditional market research methodologies, it's inexpensive and fast. In-depth analysis, of course, requires more time and expertise, and there are companies that will gladly provide those services.

Keyword research is done for several reasons, so tailor your time and effort to your current needs:

- Paid advertising on search engines is the primary driver for keyword research tools and services. Paid advertising is found on the top and right sides of the search results page—that's the money that pays for the search engine infrastructure, so you can search for free. It's also called sponsored results. This type of advertising has become popular since the number of clicks (metrics) can be measured to develop a Return on Investment (ROI) calculation. It's one of the few ways of measuring advertising effectiveness. Large organizations buy advertising on thousands of keywords using "industrial strength" keyword management services.

- Competitive intelligence is another driver for keyword research. This involves looking at both the advertising on the top and right sides of search results, as well as the natural results from the search query. This tells you the terms companies are bidding on to appear on the results page, as well as the words they are optimizing on the web pages on their websites.

- Copy writing is the primary reason I use keyword research. I want to match the words that searchers are using to the answers that are being provided. If I am crafting a title (and that is the most important element online as well as offline), it's preferable to use a highly-used synonym rather than a low-usage term. The examples below indicate that "domain" and "domain names" should both be used in my web copy for this book.

Let's look at an example of what this data looks like using a free tool from Wordtracker, one of the early keyword services. Their paid services are more extensive, and available on an affordable monthly or annual basis. The free tool can be found at:

Since the title of this book includes the word "domain," I'm interested in how the word is being used by searchers. The absolute numbers are irrelevant, since this is based on sampling, but the relative position shows popularity ranking. The first 20 results are shown below:

18,760 searches (Top 100 only)	
Searches	Keyword
18,760	total searches
1849	domain names
1538	public domain movies
1391	kids domain
744	domain name
743	domain
686	public domain music
587	public domain
522	domain registration
486	domain name registration

Searches	Keyword
460	domain name search
454	domain hosting
385	free domain name
331	eminent domain
297	domain name ip
274	domain name owner
268	free domain
259	who owns domain name
249	car domain
233	domains
217	public domain pictures

Google Adwords provides a publicly-available tool at
https://adwords.google.com/select/KeywordToolExternal   which
provides different results and numbers. These results are based on advertiser competition and relevance as determined by Google (it doesn't include other search engines). I can even look at the average Cost per Click (CPC), which is an indicator of value of the placement on Google search results pages.

Keywords	Advertiser Competition ⑦	Approx Search Volume: August ⑦	Approx Avg Search Volume ⑦
Keywords related to term(s) entered - sorted by relevance ⑦			
domain		5,000,000	5,000,000
domain registration		368,000	368,000
domain names		1,000,000	673,000
register domain		301,000	201,000
cheap domain		165,000	110,000
name domain		1,000,000	1,000,000
domain hosting		368,000	301,000
domain search		90,500	90,500
free domain		246,000	201,000
web domain		301,000	246,000
buy domain		74,000	74,000
register domain name		201,000	110,000
domain name registration		165,000	165,000
domain name search		40,500	40,500
whois domain		22,200	22,200
domain check		22,200	22,200
com domain		135,000	110,000
domain registry		22,200	22,200
register a domain		135,000	60,500
cheap domain name		40,500	33,100
register a domain name		135,000	49,500
purchase domain name		8,100	9,900
cheap domain names		33,100	22,200

Keyword research can be quite fascinating, and it's easy to spend a lot of time exploring what might work for you. I start out with single word nouns, and then explore related phrases. If you are doing extensive analysis, the commercial services are well worth the convenience of being able to build spreadsheets.

TIP Keywords, while important, may be limited in usefulness for your particular website. Keyword research is more useful for purposes that can be described by nouns, rather than general topics.

Keywords and technical structure of the web page provide the crucial foundation for your website. These are known as on-page factors in findability for your website. There are, however, off-page factors which contribute to findability of your website, and that's what we will talk about in the next chapter.

7 Making Your Site Easier to Find with Links

Why are Links Important?

Findability is more than a presence in the search engines. In the offline world, you would have referrals and directory listings. For example, the telephone directory has your phone number and street address so other people can find you. In the online world, you'll use links to your website, which can be embedded in an email, posted in a directory, or included in a blog posting.

You will recognize links that have the full URL. To illustrate with an example: http://www.econtentstrategies.com/writing.html is the web page on my consulting site with articles that I have written. On that web page, you will see a citation:

- "Promoting Information and Search Skills", Feature article, Free Pint, No. 185, June 30, 2005

The blue link is called "anchor text," and behind the scenes the article referenced with this link is actually found at:

http://www.freepint.com/issues/300605.htm#feature/

Even though the anchor text for the link could be coded a different color, we've learned to recognize blue as standard for active links.

This is the code for my web page, which was automatically generated by my HTML editor:

```
<li>

<a href="http://www.freepint.com/issues/300605.htm#feature/" tar-
get="_blank">"Promoting Information and Search Skills"</a>,
Feature article, <span style="font-style: italic;">Free Pint</span>,
No. 185, June 30, 2005<br>

</li>
```

NOTE The http:// links have to remain the same to continue to work. If Free Pint decided to change the URL structure for issues they have already published, then this link to their web page would fail. How many times have you gotten a "404 Error, Page Not Found?" The page moved to another location or was deleted, so it disappeared and can't be found.

TIP If you are citing a blog post, be sure to click through to the permalink (permanent Link). It will be either at the bottom of the post or you can click the title. Use the permalink for your reference, not the URL of the blog page where it was posted.

Maintaining permanent links should be a primary concern when structuring the website for your domain. Forwarding from old URL addresses to new addresses using redirects is possible to a limited extent, but only for those domain names that you control. This is particularly problematic with free Blogger websites that have a structure, such as: http://yourblog.blogspot.com/your-post-title.html. So, if I decide to get a web host, and import my Blogger postings into Wordpress, my postings would become http://www.mydomain.com/blog/my-post-title.html or something similar, which is not the same URL address. So you can see the importance of selecting software services that allow you to use your own domain, not theirs.

Now for the technical piece: The Free Pint URL above is an example of an outbound link to someone else's web page. I control this link on my web page, and can change or delete it as the website evolves. Within my website, I also use links to navigate between the web pages. This is what the HTML code looks like for the links at the top of my web pages:

```
<table id="toplinks">

    <tr>

    <td><a href="services.html">Services</a></td>

    <td><a href="writing.html">Writing</a></td>

    <td><a href="speaking.html">Speaking</a></td>

    <td><a href="press.html">Press</a></td>

    <td><a href="about.html">About</a></td>

    </tr>

</table>
```

Inbound links are different, and play a key role in findability of your website. These are links from other websites to your website, and you don't have control over them, since they reside on other people's domains. Of course, if you have multiple websites and multiple domains, you can link between these to a reasonable extent.

Links play an important role in search engines. Google has the infamous Page Rank algorithm that evaluates the number and quality of inbound links to your web pages, as well as other factors. It is used to rank the results presented on the search results page discussed earlier.

This patented process is based on standard scientific analysis originating in the 1960's with ISI's Science Citation Index (paper at that point). Basically, in scholarly publishing, highly-cited works are considered more authoritative. Certain publications are also considered more authoritative, based on discipline.

Let's see how this translates into the web world. There are two major pieces:

- Total number of inbound links to your website from other websites. This grows over time, which means that older websites tend to have more inbound links. It's also a reason that new websites can have a difficult time ranking high on the search results pages, particularly in competitive areas. Aged links can have high value, another reason to avoid changing URL addresses.

  On the other hand, breaking news from news feeds and blogs does not have inbound references, so these web pages are indexed separately and displayed in most current order, which is standard for premium content search engines.

- Quality of the sources of the inbound links. Just as a print article from *The New England Journal of Medicine* carries more authority than one from Prevention magazine, the same rules apply in the web world. If I were looking at a search results page, I would recognize the different sources from the URL, and click through on the one that fit my information needs. This same type of evaluation occurs algorithmically in the search engines. Educational sources, such as universities, with .edu domains carry more authority, as do many non-profits with .org domains.

There is a whole specialty of Search Engine Optimization (SEO) professionals with expertise in this area. They keep up-to-date on the constantly-changing landscape of search engine marketing. Ranking for search results is a cat-and-mouse game between the search engines and spammers, which mean the algorithms are constantly tweaked.

From a practical standpoint, you can follow a few rules that will give you the usual 80% effectiveness with 20% of the work:

- Clearly state the purpose and value of each and every page in your website, and provide internal links to the rest of the site for more information. There has to be a reason for someone else to link to one of your web pages, and typically it's not the top level of your website. Links to resource pages are quite popular, bypassing your home page. The messaging has to be clear, as does usability. Yes, attractive design helps too, but there are lots of Plain Jane websites and even ugly websites that do their job well.

- Use the language that other people use, identified by keyword research. This is a best practice. Use these keywords as anchor text for links as well as titles. Remember that marketing jargon can muddy communication.

- Develop links naturally. Websites should have a balance of inbound and outbound links. I have outbound links to articles written for publications, and I have inbound links from associations that I belong to as well as my profiles on the San Jose State University website, and LinkedIn. Just like real life networks, links for a real estate agent will be different than those for a consultant.

Now let's look at developing those *oh-so-important* inbound links....

How Are Links Developed?

Links can be ephemeral—an email from a friend, a mention in a print newsletter, or simply word of mouth. Permanent links, however, are more desirable since they accumulate. They are actually semi-permanent, as links do get corrupted over time.

Directories

In print form, directories are a very traditional source of finding people, services, and businesses. Think of the White and Yellow Pages, university faculty listings, United Way organization directories, and a multitude of other types of directories that help you locate what you are looking for. The good news is directory functionality has moved online, with the benefit of more frequent updates since changes can be made on an ongoing basis, rather than tied to a printing schedule.

Directories for professional organizations can be an excellent means of improving visibility, both through incoming links to your sites and by including your profile on the organization's website. Web addresses can now be added to the usual titles, descriptions, addresses and phone numbers. Your URL in a directory can provide an inbound link for your website, in addition to visibility in the directory itself.

Printed directories are organized into distinct categories, and typically restrict your listing to only one category. Online, your listing can be in multiple categories, and even more importantly, most online directories include search capabilities.

Consider directories as simply a collection of names and addresses (either physical or web) with additional information. LinkedIn can be considered a directory, and when you add your websites to your public profile, you get another inbound link to your website.

TIP Be sure to use the Other websites category on LinkedIn so you can put a keyword phrase in the anchor text, rather than "My Company" website.

There are blog directories, special interest directories (also called portals), local directories, and industry directories—just find those that are appropriate for your purposes. Time, energy, and your checkbook are additional factors in choosing how many and which directories to use. Many of the web sources are free, and can be real budget savers. Association memberships typically include directory listings with membership. You know how those fees can add up!

Reviews

Product reviews, book reviews and restaurant reviews have been offline staples for years, and have been highly sought after for the free publicity they generated. However, the reviews were generally done by professionals and had relatively limited distribution channels.

New web technology has opened up new venues for reviews which have the same benefits (visibility) and downsides (poor reviews) as the traditional process. User-generated reviews (also known as User Generated Content or UGC) can be moderated, but may also be unmoderated.

Yelp.com is an example of a website that provides both a directory of local services, and an opportunity for individuals to post a review. Zagat's print restaurant review guide has now migrated to the web. Amazon allows reviews of their products, and you can even establish a profile to include a link to your website, though it doesn't appear to be live. Check out the many review sites, especially those relevant to your site, for additional sources of inbound links.

Review bias can be problematic. As a consumer, I value comments from actual users of products and services. There have been cases where companies paid for positive reviews, a not-unknown practice in the offline world also. Definitely consider using something like Google Alerts or a reputation management service to monitor postings on the web mentioning your website, both negative and positive.

Commenting

In the offline world, letters to the editor are well-accepted editorial practice. In the web world, letters to the editor can take the form of commenting on discussion boards, forums, blogs and news stories. All of these can increase your online visibility. Start by reading those sites of interest to you, then commenting on the postings. Most sites that encourage comments have moderators, or require a login, to combat spam.

Because online does not have the limitation of physical page space, the number of reviews is not limited. Online, you can post as many comments as you have time and interest to pursue. Signature lines are a must for this environment and should include your domain name for a link back to your site. Be careful about exposing your actual email since these can be harvested by spammers.

You need to contribute meaningful comment to the community that hangs out online. Typically, you will find a handful of regular posters who are opinion leaders, in addition to the moderator. Most people are lurkers, with a number of occasional posters on the active communities. These postings can have a long life. My comments on Wikipedia to a licensing group in 2005 still show up in a search by my name; I have even found comments dating back to 2000.

Articles and Press Mentions

Writing articles has been a time-tested way to get personal or organizational visibility. Articles written for an established print publication can have the benefit of appearing both in print, and online, as well as in aggregated content repositories. Online articles can be part of electronic newsletters and can also be posted on websites.

The publications you target for your articles will depend on the audience you are targeting and what they are reading. For general distribution, you can submit to article directories to increase distribution. Check out the article directory's requirements and restrictions on duplicate content. Get full online benefit by including a resource box with your name and website.

Press mentions are another well-established means to establish credibility and visibility. I have been interviewed by various publications. For example, Entrepreneur.com interviewed me back in 2000, about establishing a home office. My name and consulting practice appeared in the article, in print and online, and the article is still available at http://tinyurl.com/62bguw.html

Online, your name and website can show up as part of a posting from a blogger who heard a presentation at a conference or read an article. Speakers are typically mentioned on the organizer's website. You may even be listed as an attendee at smaller conferences, so this is another means of visibility. I went to the 2007 WordCamp, a workshop on Wordpress, in San Francisco, and my name was included on the list of attendees.

Some of these mentions will include a live link back to your website (best), but generally any publicity is good. Of course, you want positive publicity. But, beware: negative publicity is as visible as positive publicity. Some publicity is annoying. Especially when you can't make changes. I used my phone number for Little League baseball signups in 2002, and it still shows up in searches, though not with my domain name.

How are Links Used in Internet Marketing?

Internet marketing is simply the use of online technologies to implement traditional marketing practices. You still need to develop an effective marketing message and identify the intended audience. The new technologies are used for delivery and follow-up. Links provide the interactivity for implementation. Let's look at how traditional marketing translates into web technologies:

Classified Advertising

Those 2–4 line ads that traditionally have appeared in the back of newspapers and magazines are the revenue goldmine on the web. Google Adwords PPC (Pay Per Click) ads, the ones on the top and right sides of search results pages, popularized this advertising format on the web. These sponsored links, meaning advertisers pay for their placement, trump the organic search results based on relevance algorithms. Placement for sponsored links is based on bids. Generally, the higher the bid, and the more money the sponsor has paid, the higher the ad appears on the page.

Here's a typical PPC ad from Google—note that the URL for the link is the top level home page, but could be to a specialized landing page with a signup or other call to action.

The advertiser pays only for clicks through to the web page, so PPC has been very popular. PPC is a self-service model—set up an online account, enter in the four lines, authorize advertising charges, and activate. No sales rep, no advertising agency, no delays, no setup costs. You can get immediate results, which is a great marketing advantage, allowing split-testing of different ads and different landing pages. Cost per click varies from nickels and dimes to more than $100. Great for small businesses, and cumbersome for large advertisers. Just be really consistent in checking your link usage, since costs can skyrocket.

You'll find this type of text link advertising on major search engines and many websites. It's relatively simple to implement, though there is an art to optimizing the limited number of characters available. Click-through rates are comparable to direct response marketing, usually less than 5%, with less than 1% not unusual, so tweaking to find the best conversion rate is standard practice.

Google has also added another form of PPC advertising called Adsense, for publishers of web pages. By embedding a snippet of HTML code on your web page, Google will "serve up" ads on your page, similar to the search results ads, labeled "Ads by Google." Revenue from these ads (Yahoo or Google or other ad networks) is shared with the owner of the web pages. This is a common way to make money with blogs, but the revenue to the blog publisher tends to be low.

The general format of classified advertising is quite flexible, and relatively low cost. Classified ads with text links are also used in electronic newsletters, called ezines, and these have live links. Print newsletters can also have web links included in their classified advertising to replace or to augment a phone number. Just like traditional ad placement, you'll decide on a workable number of websites for your marketing efforts.

Display Advertising

Internet marketers call these banner ads, and they were the primary revenue generators for websites and search engines before the advent of PPC ads. The big difference is that they are typically priced on a number of times displayed basis (called CPM), rather than a click-through basis.

Advertisers shifted from banners to PPC, but banners have now increased in popularity for brand advertising. Banner advertising allows more creative than text advertising, but the implementation is a bit more complex than the self-service text model. Banners can be implemented in different ways: static ads, pop-ups, pop-unders or animated.

The URL link is typically hidden behind the creative, so it is activated after you click on the ad. News sites tend to have a lot of banner advertising, which complements their print advertising.

Direct Response Marketing

Direct marketing is very effective in the offline world—that's what fills up our email inboxes! From a marketing standpoint, the online direct marketing takes a much shorter time and is less expensive to implement than offline alternatives.

Automatic email follow-up, known as autoresponder services, are an underappreciated marketing tool. Vacation notices that we can set on our own email accounts are the simplest form of autoresponder. E-commerce sites have more extensive autoresponder messages which track the progress of your order with different notifications. Amazon built their early success on these types of messages, which built confidence in the online ordering process.

Sequential autoresponder services are similar and may be part of an e-commerce shopping cart package. These services, however, are also provided by specialized email delivery companies. The attraction of these services is that a series of email messages can be created and delivered over a period of time, which can be months long.

For marketing purposes, this is the equivalent of mailing a series of marketing pieces, a standard practice in direct marketing. Online delivery means the readers can click a link to go to a web page, providing interactivity and trackability. Delivery costs are lower, and feedback more immediate.

Once created, the autoresponder series is triggered by either an email opt-in or by signing up at your website. This means no manual follow-up, and starts the series when a user opts-in, not when the mailing house sends out the collateral and it gets delivered to a snail mailbox.

You've probably seen autoresponders in action without realizing what they were. Some examples of emails sent by autoresponder services:

- You've requested a white paper or special report about a topic by filling in a form, and getting an email with the link to download the PDF. This not only verifies your email address and improve the odds of ending up in your email box, but allows the author to track who is getting the report and provides a channel for follow up with interested recipients.

- You've signed up for an email course to be delivered over a period of weeks.

- You registered for a conference, and then get pre-conference notifications, a post-conference survey and nine months later, receive an invitation to register with special alumni pricing.

- You've noticed an email address in a resource box in a print publication to request more information, which is automatically delivered.

The other major service that these companies provide is delivery of electronic newsletters and broadcast messages to mailing lists. If you look at the bottom of newsletters that you receive, you'll notice the unsubscribe links which go back to these services to remove you automatically from the email list.

These services exist because managing email lists is tedious. Subscribe/unsubscribe is a clerical function that can be automated. Optimizing delivery to the plethora of different domains and email addresses is overwhelming, best done by a specialized service.

From a domain point of view, it's always best to have email marketing originate with a service, rather than your domain name. Spam is a huge problem, and your domain may inadvertently be tagged as a spam originator. It is easier to switch email delivery services than to convince Google and Yahoo that your site is not an offender.

Offline/Online Integrated Campaigns

This is the buzz phrase used by traditional marketers when they realized the internet couldn't be ignored. Internet marketers came from the online-only world, and traditional marketers came from the traditional media world. In the early days of the web, the battle was to get website URLs included on marketing and product collateral. Marketers now include URLs everywhere—even my exercise ball has a URL.

Now there is a greater understanding of the strengths of traditional media vs. the strengths of online media. Online web pages have replaced sending out informational packages, reducing costs and providing immediate delivery. Postcards with a URL to a special offer page have become an effective way of reaching an audience defined by buying a snail mailing list, based on certain demographics. Radio ads often include a website domain name that needs to be easy to say and remember.

Networking and Referrals

Social media has become the darling of the web world. Though it has a new label, it's basically technology applied to day-to-day human behavior. We all exist in a community, whether it's Little League, our local school, Rotary, or a professional organization.

Now we can participate electronically in these communities, as well as others that are worldwide, using various tools. You can join an email list, which allows you to send and receive emails from all the members. Yahoo Groups is popular example of these services, called listservs. Some listserv groups are very active, and others hardly at all.

MySpace and Facebook are an expansion of the same behaviors, but allow multiple groups within a total collection of contacts. These companies started with teenagers and college students, but have become mainstream for adults.

Word of mouth has always been a powerful force, whether it's about the latest movie or latest Apple product. Now called viral marketing, it can be as simple as an email from a friend with a link to an interesting web page. It's become very effective by linking and commenting on blog posts.

Referrals are golden in the offline world—the source of jobs, sales, friends, and resources. Referrals are particularly trusted when they come from others you trust. The same is true in the online world. Referrals have become an important part of social media websites. LinkedIn allows you to write recommendations for people. Del.icio.us allows you to bookmark websites you consider interesting and share them with others. Flickr allows you to post photos publicly and YouTube lets you post videos. You can then share these photos and videos with other people by sending them favorite links.

As these networks grow, your email with your permanent domain name becomes more important in staying connected. Some services, such as LinkedIn, allow you to have multiple emails, which means changing to another email is doable. In others, you have to unsubscribe with the old email, and then resubscribe with the new email, which can mean losing history and reputation.

Overwhelmed by the detail and number of options? There are learning curves for learning web technology, and it just takes a while to understand how the pieces fit together. Next, let's look at the steps to do that.

Chapter 7: Making Your Site Easier to Find with Links

8 Action Plan for Your Domain Name

Now that you've gotten an overview of establishing a web presence using your own domain name, it's time to implement. The key is tackling manageable pieces, and completing them one at a time. It's just like remodeling or building a home; you can't do everything at once. You can be working on different phases at the same time, just as you are collecting lighting fixture ideas while framing and hanging sheetrock.

Phase 1: Register Your Domain

Estimated Time: 1–2 hours

Ongoing: Review quarterly for renewals and adjustments.

Domain registration is the most clearly defined stage. You find available domain names, web addresses, using a recommended domain registrar. It's just like looking for property for sale or development, and requires some research. Then you register domain names under your name, and set up payments. Follow the advice in Chapter 2 on selecting different options.

If you haven't registered a domain, then register a domain name that is a variant of your personal name. Defer research on business names to a different phase which involves setting up your online business and website. Once you understand the process, it's easy to register additional domain names, particularly for special purposes.

If you already own a domain name (or several), then log on to your registrar and bring the information up-to-date. Is the email current? Are you using a permanent email that you check regularly, not the domain email? Who is listed as owner, billing and technical contact? What are the renewal dates?

Then plan for ongoing review. Who is responsible for making the annual payments? This is particularly problematic for volunteer organizations. The officers change from year to year, and the treasurer may not be aware of the annual payments, since there is no paper invoice to be routed to a P.O. box for the organization. My local Bobbie Sox league lost their domain name due to payment snafus, and the domain was snatched up by a domain squatter, and ultimately used for a pornography site.

Automatic renewal is good, but you'll need to decide whether you want to keep your domain names. I used to register the .org and .net variants of my .com domains, but no longer keep those. Perhaps you registered a domain for a possible business, but changed your mind on the business name.

Print off the list of domains, and the setup information, along with the login information. I put these in my 3-ring binder labeled "Important Technical Stuff." The login information goes into a 3-ring page protector that I can identify quickly for quarterly review.

Now find the email forwarding options, the URL forwarding options and the DNS screens. You may need to update them based on decisions made in the following phases.

At a minimum, you need to look at the default web page for your URL. This is the "Under Construction" page you may have seen for some URLs, but it can be a page full of links that are generating money for the registrar. One colleague had registered a domain name and discovered to her horror that it was defaulting to adult content links.

A best practice is to have a generic web page that you can use for URL forwarding for parked domain names that you own. You can use LinkedIn or some other social media profile. Or if you have an existing website, have a web page that is not linked to the rest of your web pages that is your version of "Under Construction." It's the equivalent of a vacant lot, and a way to control the information from web surfers. Do you want to allow advertising on that lot? If so, then you should be in control, not defaulting to your registrar.

3LS PROJECT

Phase 2: Set Up Your Email

Estimated time: 1–4 hours

Ongoing: Monitor daily for workability, adjust as needed

Your day-to-day email configuration is usually the most urgent phase of using your domain name. You'll want to put an email with your domain name on business cards, and use in your usual email communications, including the signature block. Stop giving out your comcast.net, gmail.com, yahoo.com, hotmail.com or other ISP email. It's not the professional look you want to have.

It takes time for people to start using your new domain name, so start notifying your network that you have a new email. You'll want to keep the old email active, just starting reminding your correspondents to use the new email. And, you'll need to unsubscribe to email lists under your old email, and resubscribe under your new domain email. The bad news is that this is tedious, but the good news is that you only have to switch to domain-based email once.

Begin this phase by deciding your primary email reader software, based on the discussion in Chapter 3. Where do you want to compose your emails? Will it be a desktop email client, typically Outlook, Outlook

Express, Thunderbird, or Apple Mail? Or will it be a web-based service, such as Gmail or Yahoo Mail? Or will you use a mail service provided by your web hosting company?

You may decide on a hybrid approach. I use a primary Gmail account to collect emails from all of my domains so I can review the spam from all of them in the same place (Google is very good at identifying spam!). I use Gmail filters to attach a label that corresponds to the domain name, so a glance at my inbox shows me all the incoming emails. I also selectively use Gmail filters to forward newsletters to a second account, to read at my leisure.

Originally, I used to download the remaining email to Outlook Express on my hard drive, then received email and sent replies (two different functions) from there. I like the threaded email capability on Gmail, so that all the email relating to a subject line are grouped together, so now I find myself simply replying on Gmail, rather than downloading to Outlook Express. I can originate email on my hard drive, and use only the send capability and cc:ing myself, so the original email ends up on Gmail.

This approach works for me since I am usually connected to the internet using a high-speed connection. If you want to do email offline, and connect only to send and receive, you will probably want to use your local desktop email reader. Tracking email receipts and setting priority features are only available on desktop email readers at this point.

Both Google and Yahoo mail are moving targets. Late in 2007, Gmail introduced IMAP capability that supposedly improves synchronization between their web mail and devices. This is particularly useful with accessing email via mobile devices. That's my next experimentation, and will be posted on the website for this book. Earlier, in 2006, Google had introduced Google Apps for small businesses with additional features for domain name email. These too may be possibilities for you.

Your website hosting company will also provide email options for you, and actual customer support. If all of your websites are hosted on the same service, then this is a good option. You should be able to access the hosting service, both via web mail and by downloading email to your local email reader. A major consideration is the level of spam filtering that can be provided by your website hosting company.

Once you have made your choices, read the email setup information that corresponds to your choices (located under Help). It has all the *oh-so-important* details needed to make your email reader work. As you set it up, be sure to utilize some overlooked capabilities:

- Always set up email accounts with a name in addition to the email address. This can be found under Properties or Account Information, depending on your mail reader software. The receiver of your email then knows who sent the email, so it doesn't look like spam. Your name will then get attached to the email address in their address book, so they can actually find your email address by using search.

- Change the default email to your primary domain name email. I use Jean@Bedord.com, so no one ever sees my gmail.com or comcast.net mail account. I can send from multiple accounts, but if I forget to change the drop-down box, the email is still recognizable as coming from me.

- Choose the following setting if it's available to keep your email accounts straight:

  When I receive a message sent to one of my addresses:

  ⊙ Reply from the same address the message was sent to

- You can specify a different Reply-To address when you set up each account. This can be useful for sending out messages from one account when you want the responses to go to another account or to someone else.

- Set up signatures for each email account. Search your email reader for the instructions. I use different signatures, depending on whether I'm replying as Professor Bedord or Jean Bedord, Findability and Search Consultant. I include a title, website, phone number and email in somewhat modified format—with spaces around the @ or spelled out. If your signature block gets indexed through social media, this is somewhat of a block to spammers. Always provide alternative ways for others to contact you. My graduate students make this mistake all the time. I get an email from GuessWhoIAm@Hotmail.com with no identifying information, either in the account name or signature. They get a firm reminder about professional email communication, as well as about meaningful subject lines.

- Multiple signature capabilities vary by email readers. Outlook Express has nice capabilities, but Gmail only allows one signature, so I have to cut and paste signature blocks. Such are the idiosyncrasies of software.

As you set up your emails, spam control is a major consideration. As described in Chapter 3, you will have emails on different computer servers. Review options carefully, and in particular, TURN OFF the "catchall" category for emails, leaving only the actual emails you set up active. This was not a problem in the early days of email, but the catchall category means any email with your domain name gets through to your reader, even if is iedhtlk@yourdomain.com. Info@yourdomain.com and webmaster@yourdomain.com are generic, and easily used by spammers. Simply provide contact information on your web pages, with the email as a web form or an image or some other format which can be read by humans, but not spam bots which read the HTML mailto: tag.

Testing is the most time consuming part of this phase, since you'll need to figure out the right combination that works for you. Send emails to friends and family, and have them reply to you. Keep notes, since you will probably end up making changes, depending on your work habits.

Phase 3: Develop Your Website

Estimated time: 1–2 days for fewer than 5 pages, with pre-existing copy; up to a few weeks if the copy has to be developed, or if the website is bigger.

Ongoing: Review every six months for static sites, post on a regular basis for blog sites.

This phase is the most variable, since it depends on the complexity of the website, just like building from the ground up or remodeling a house. Unlike bricks-and-mortar, it's relatively easy to redesign your website (no permits required!), so the key is to get something developed as a starter site, then go back and rework. A 1–5 page starter site can expand to 15–20 pages as more content is added. Adding a blog to an existing website is relatively straightforward, either hosted or on your web hosting service.

The key is keeping the URLs constant, although the web pages themselves can change. It's no different than furnishing a room with essential furniture, then adding accessories over time as time and budget allow. Just as you can plan on adding additional rooms to a starter home, so you can add additional web pages to a starter website. The key is planning for change.

This phase begins with deciding on the type of website you want for your domain, based on the overview provided in Chapter 4. Then you'll need to do the planning described in Chapter 5 so that you know the approximate number of web pages that need to be developed. These two steps will give you a good idea of whether to do-it-yourself, subcontract some of the job, or hire a general contractor to create the entire website.

You'll need to evaluate your copywriting skills and technical skills, plus the complexity of the site you want developed. The one-page website that you need for domain forwarding in phase one can simply be the information on your business card, with contact information and the purpose of the domain. A more elaborate one-page website would be the equivalent of a handout you use for networking purposes.

I write my own copy, but you can hire someone to convert your writing to web style copy writing which is similar to newspaper writing, with short paragraphs and keyword optimized sentences. Copywriters are not graphic designers and they are not programmers, so evaluating skillset is important in hiring expertise.

It's easy to assume one person can handle all the different aspects, but the perspectives are different. Habits can also be a factor, since best practices change with new tools and the changing search landscape. Always check out portfolios and recommendations to find compatibilities, and most important, become knowledgeable yourself so you can determine whether the website will work for you, the website owner. I also recommend learning some basic HTML, which makes troubleshooting easier. You'll recognize clean, well-organized code, just as you recognize work by a good finish carpenter (not the framing carpenter).

Simple websites can be developed quickly, and hiring a professional to complete the publication to a website host can make this go even more rapidly. I find trying to fix technical glitches and ensuring browser compatibilities is a time sink, so I tend to hire some technical expertise to finish the project. By that point, I just want to get it done and working.

Larger and more complex websites can take much longer. Just like construction, the key to faster implementation and cost containment is clear decisions up-front and written details. Planning on index cards is cost-effective—it's much cheaper to make changes with pen and pencil. Web professionals and programmers are like building contractors—it's expensive and time consuming to keep making changes. They get really cranky if you keep changing your mind, and the change orders pile up. Knowing the jargon also helps—you need to learn to understand, if not speak their language (See Chapter 5).

Once you have a web page of some sort, even if it is just URL forwarding at your registrar to LinkedIn or some other social media page, you can put the URL on your business card and in your signature block. Putting together a social media profile is probably a two-hour job, if you are working from an existing resume or copy. It may take twice that if you don't have a current resume.

Phase 4: Link Building & Social Media

Estimated time: 1–2 hours for initial evaluation, ongoing 1–2 hours per week.

This is the most open-ended phase, and needs ongoing attention if you want to build web traffic to your website. The approaches you take depend on the audience and community that you are trying to reach. A website for a bricks-and-mortar business will focus on local listings, whereas a consultant may focus on an industry.

Start this phase immediately after registering a domain name, setting up your email and an initial web page. It takes time to build inbound links, so the sooner you start, the more links you will build. You can hire internet marketers to build links on your behalf, but I recommend doing at least part of them yourself to get an understanding of the dynamics.

As discussed in Chapter 6, the first step in making your site visible on the web is getting into the search engine indexes. Inclusion is not automatic, so you need to get some inbound links to help Google, Yahoo and other search engines find your site.

Start by evaluating your current associations and services. Do they have profiles that allow a link to your website? Are you involved with a non-profit, as a volunteer or sponsor? Are there community or industry directories where your website can be included? Do you belong to a Chamber of Commerce or a local service organization, such as Rotary? Is your business included in the online yellow pages and other local business directories?

Online press releases work very well for businesses since they provide authority and immediacy, as well as live links. Blogs also provide immediacy since they are set up to notify the search engines of new posts via ping servers. Both press releases and blog posts are monitored by traditional media, which may provide additional publicity.

Chapter 7 provides an overview of link building and social media opportunities. Identify two or three which are most appropriate for your audience, and focus on those. Just like any type of marketing, these activities take time, energy and/or money to implement. You'll need to build link building and promotion into your everyday workflow, and add new approaches over time.

Don't overlook the obvious—using your new domain email to send out emails to your friends, family and colleagues with the new website. Include your new domain email and website in a signature block on every email you send.

Building a web presence is a process that takes time to develop. The DNS (domain name system) was invented in the early 1980s, over twenty-five years ago, and is now utilized in ways never envisioned by the original researchers. The search engine environment dominated by Google has just evolved in the last ten years. Social media is even more recent—LinkedIn was founded in 2002, MySpace in 2003, Facebook and Flickr in 2004, and YouTube in 2005.

Utilizing your own domain name effectively in this ecosystem requires mastering the technology basics as well as following the evolution of the web environment. As someone who grew up with the evolution of computers from mainframes, the flexibility and usefulness of the technology continues to impress me! Enjoy building....

About the Author

Jean Bedord left her corporate job nearly ten years ago to gain flexibility for her family life. Configuring personal technology for her consulting work proved challenging, even though she had spent nearly twenty years working in technology and online information product development. As more of her friends and colleagues become solo professionals and entrepreneurs, they need guides to help navigate the same maze. As Jean found, they expect the same functionality provided within the corporate infrastructure, but that requires selecting technology for their new environment.

Jean has multiple lives and multiple domains. Her corporate consulting practice can be found at http://www.econtentstrategies.com. She is also a workshop instructor and part-time faculty at San Jose State University graduate School of Library and Information Science. Her website http://www.CorporateNoMore.com is designed to empower individuals so they can effectively utilize technologies outside the corporate environment.

Her recommendations for web services can be found at www.JustAskJean.com.

Create Thought Leadership for your Company

Books deliver instant credibility to the author. Having an MBA or Ph.D. is great; however, putting the word "author" in front of your name is similar to using the letters Ph.D. or MBA. You are no long Michael Green, you are "Author Michael Green."

Books give you a platform to stand on. They help you to:

- Demonstrate your thought leadership
- Generate leads

Books deliver increased revenue, particularly indirect revenue:

- A typical consultant will make 3x in indirect revenue for every dollar they make on book sales

Books are better than a business card. They are:

- More powerful than white papers
- An item that makes it to the book shelf vs. the circular file
- The best tschocke you can give at a conference

Why Wait to Write Your Book?

Check out other companies that have built credibility by writing and publishing a book through Happy About

Contact Happy About at 408-257-3000 or go to http://happyabout.com.

Other Happy About® Books

Purchase these books at Happy About
http://happyabout.com
or at other online and physical bookstores.

DNA of the Young Entrepreneur

This personal narrative distills wisdom from the author's self-made journey from poverty to wealth.

Paperback $34.95
eBook $11.95

42 Rules of Social Media For Business

A modern survival guide to effective social media communications, written from first-hand experience.

Paperback: $19.95
eBook: $11.95

Networking Online- Making LinkedIn Work for you!

This book explains the benefits of using LinkedIn and recommends best practices so that you can get the most out of it.

Paperback: $19.95
eBook: $11.95

I'm on Facebook—Now What???

This book shows you how to get Business and Professional Value from Facebook

Paperback $19.95
eBook $11.95

Additional Praise for this book

"If you're a business owner expanding to the web—or someone looking to start a business online—you'll find this book helpful and enlightening. It provides a guide to deciphering the jargon and making the decisions that keep many people from achieving Online Success. Read this book first, then invest in tools and technology that fit your needs. Even if you've been in business online for a while, I recommend you review this book—there are insights you may have missed when you got started."
Jeanette S Cates, PhD, The Technology Tamer™
OnlineSuccessCoaching.com & YourInternetStrategist.com

"Getting on the Internet can be a challenge for individuals and small business owners who don't have the luxury of an in-house IT staff who know all of the mysteries of domains and email and web sites. Jean's book answers all the questions you have, and gives you great background for getting your own Internet address—your domain—as well as a professional email. She also tells you what you need to get a web site or blog up and running, and how you can make sure that friends and customers can find you with Google and the other internet search giants.
The book also gives you a task-oriented action plan that takes you through the complete process, so you'll be up and running professionally in minimum time. A great book to keep on the bookshelf!"
Miles Kehoe, President, New Idea Engineering Inc., http://ideaeng.com

"This book is clearly, understandably, and straightforwardly written and should be read by anyone who is planning a website. It contains not just information that beginners need, but a lot of practical and valuable information that many people who have had domain names for quite a while may not have considered. It is a quick, easy read with a balanced combination of both the "how's" and the "why's," including a number of important facets that no website builder should risk missing or ignoring. If you are a new or even not-new owner of a domain name, this book will be well worth your time."
Randolph Hock, Ph.D., Online Strategies and Author, http://onstrat.com **&** http://extremesearcher.com/

"This book is very useful for cultivating new clients. Once they understand the steps involved in establishing their web presence, the value of my consulting services is more obvious. They have a better understanding of what they can do themselves, and which services they want to outsource to professionals. We can then talk a common language and get the website they need to support their business much faster."
Pat Wiklund, Consultant, 1personbusiness.com